VESTA TILLEY

Sara Maitland

Published by VIRAGO PRESS Limited 1986
41 William IV Street, London WC2N 4DB

Copyright © Sara Maitland 1986

British Library Cataloguing in Publication Data

Maitland, Sara
   Vesta Tilley. − (Virago pioneers)
   1. Tilley, Vesta   2. Entertainers − Great Britain
   − Biography
   I. Title
   792.7′028′0924   PN2598.T57

   ISBN 0−86068−795−3

Typeset by Florencetype Limited, Bristol
Printed in Great Britain by Anchor Brendon,
Tiptree, Essex

CONTENTS

ACKNOWLEDGEMENTS

This book is dedicated to my daughter Mildred, simply because she has so much flash; and to her friends in the hope that they will all grow up with a clearer understanding of the social construction of gender and therefore better chances to change it.

I would like to thank the many people who have helped me with this book, especially Mandy Merck whose generosity with her own ideas and work is nearly as extraordinary as her conversation; Ursula Owen who solicited the book; Diana Simmonds whose thoughts on male-impersonation were provocative and useful; Michela Richardson who raised the questions; David Randall, Sue Dowell, Christopher Back, Maggie Lawrence, Anne McDermid, Ruthie Petrie, Colin Boswell.

I would also like to thank the Theatre Museum at the Victoria & Albert, and Joseph Mitcheson and Colin Mabberley at the Manders and Mitcheson Theatre Museum for their helpfulness and knowledge.

The photographs are reproduced by kind permission of the following: BBC Hulton Picture Library, 'The Modern Girl'; *Collection Viollet*, George Sand; Circus World Museum, Josephine/Joseph; *Communist Party Picture Library*, Elsie James and Jessie Kenney; *Harlingue-Viollet*, Colette; *Mander and Mitchenson*, Dan Leno and Vesta Tilley as principal boy; *National Film Archive*, Marlene Deitrich and Greta Garbo; *Victoria and Albert Theatre Museum*, Sarah Bernhardt, Dan Leno and all of the publicity postcards of Vesta Tilley.

CHRONOLOGY

13 May 1864	Vesta Tilley, born Matilda Powles, in Worcester, second child of Harry Powles (later Ball) and Matilda Broughton Powles.
1867	Harry P.les takes job as Chairman at the Theatre Royal, Gloucester.
1868	She makes her first stage appearance at a benefit for her father.
1870	She does her first male-impersonation as 'The Pocket Sim Reeves'.
1875	She makes her London debut at the Canterbury, Lambeth. Changes her stage name from 'The Great Little Tilley' to Vesta Tilley.
1877	First Pantomime season, Portsmouth.
1881	First Drury Lane Pantomime (she plays Second Boy to Nellie Power).
1889	Her father dies.
16 August 1890	Marries Walter de Frece, second son of Henry de Frece, the Liverpool Music Hall owner, at Brixton Registry Office, London.
1890–92	Ill. Hereafter, she and Walter de Frece spend some months every year in the South of France, usually in Monte Carlo or Monaco.
1894	First trip to America. She opens at Pastors. (Further trips are made in 1896,

	1897–8, 1901, 1903 and 1906. She tours her own Vaudeville company in 1897–8 and her own play *Algy* in 1903.)
1907	Music Hall strike.
1 July 1912	Royal Command Variety Performance.
1914	Outbreak of war.
12 July 1919	Walter de Frece knighted.
August 1919	She begins her farewell tour.
1920	Walter de Frece wins Ashton-under-Lyme at a by-election.
6 June 1920	Vesta Tilley's farewell performance. Ellen Terry presents her with 'The People's Tribute', signed by nearly two million fans.
1923	She is presented at Court.
1924	Walter de Frece becomes MP for Blackpool.
1932	Walter de Frece retires. They go to live in Monte Carlo.
8 January 1935	Walter de Frece dies in Monte Carlo. Vesta Tilley continues to live there.
16 September 1952	On a rare visit to London, at Arlington House, Vesta Tilley dies.

The Man: You can't do what's not natural; nobody can.
The Woman: And louts like you have nature in your pocket?
  Lascelles Abercrombie

It is only shallow people who do not judge by appearances.
  Oscar Wilde

OVERTURE

" In the early days of the women's movement (roughly speaking, from Mrs Bloomer to Lady Harberton) it was the whim of advanced female reformers to dress up as men. Several of my friends had that whim, one of them (poor girl) acted on it, and wore a high stiff collar that sawed her neck, and the most atrocious baggy knickerbockers! She was a horror to look upon. I found it difficult − in spite of my careful upbringing − to refrain from profanity. She used to ask me why I objected. There were several reasons, most of which I did not want to tell her, but my one triumphant argument, whereto she had no answer, save a shrug of the shoulders that sent the edge of her collar cutting into her pretty neck, was this: If all you women take to trousers, there's an end for good and all to Vesta Tilley.

Vesta Tilley! most perfect of mashers, most charming of women! What would we not give to keep you swaggering in your trimly-fitting clothes across the London boards?

When Vesta Tilley is on the bill you had best book far in advance, or you may tiptoe disconsolately at the back of the 'standing room', and catch but a stray glimpse of the goddess through the bobbing leafage of ladies' hats. Say you have been wise and have got a seat in row D of the stalls, where you will not lose the slightest of her gestures. You have dozed through clown and conjuror and operatic antique . . . And now . . .

Almost before you have looked at your programme the electric-lit numbers that flank the footlights have twitched and changed, and the band is playing a merry dancing chorus you know. A ripple of applause grows to thunder and dies away in the gallery . . . And the orchestra plays the chorus through again, for Vesta Tilley — artful fellow — loves to keep us waiting and expectant!

There is the low buzz of a bell, the conductor bends to his orchestra, the chorus starts again, and a dapper young man in an exquisite purple holiday costume strolls from the wings, leaning on his bending cane. He comes to the centre of the footlights, and poses with crossed legs and staring monocle, the features deliciously quizzical and inane. It is a perfect picture — perfect in colour and composition, the quintessence of seaside dandyism; but for a subtle hint of womanly waist and curving hips you might fancy it indeed a round-faced boy. Even so, you are doubtful.

And then the picture speaks, and the illusion is piquantly broken — or, rather, the optical illusion continues, only there is another person present: the woman artist who unfolds the tale.

In deliberate, confidential recitative she tells us of Bertie, the thirty-bob clerk, who sweats in a London office for fifty-one weeks of the year, and for this one blessed week is lording it on the Brighton promenade as the mashaw (and she shoots her cuffs) — er — Claude de Vere. Exquisite caricature! Every gesture is right; every tone is right — striking the delicate chord between irony and burlesque; there is no weak exuberance, everything is done with a fine, virile restraint. These are not quite the gestures a dandy clerk would make; they are better than that — they explain him, laugh at him, justify him. They have all the deep truth of uncynical humour. Dickens would have written a story round this fellow and called him Mr Guppy.

And the gestures move to rhythm — the strut, the cocking of the hat, the dusting of the clothes and boots with the purple handkerchief, the throwing of stones into water from the pier — pier — pier, all the ironic melody controls. Is it a dainty, flitting butterfly you are looking at or an affected fop? Perhaps, seen from this proper distance, they are the same.

How sure the singer is! How despotically she rules over her audience — dallies with the rhythm, draws it out, pauses in mid-gesture, the hand in the air, the monocle nearing the eye — pauses perilously long, you get uneasy, the bicycle goes so slow you are afraid it will topple — it almost does — but in good time the chorus comes to its conclusion with a 'My word!' and one dainty, feminine hand slaps the other, and the body wriggles into itself with a foot up. 'My word! He — is — a naugh — ty boy!' O Tilley! Tilley! How you know us and our little foibles! . . . And all the while, for all her truth to masculine type, you get a sense of the feminine, not as with those clumsy imitators of hers who are giggling women in thin disguise, but just so much that the truth of the male gesture is made the more piquant by that hint of curving shape. And yet her soul is the soul of a boy — or perhaps, shall I say, of a girl, at the age when girls and boys are very much alike. She is and always will be a naive child. *"*

(*Taken from* W.R. Titterton, *From Theatre to Music Hall*, p. 145, Stephen Swift & Co., London, 1912)

BEGINNERS

We pry into the lives and times of others partly because we are
nosy — but also because we do not want to go on the same . . .
that is if we seek an approach to history that is at once both
critical and revolutionary.

Sheila Rowbotham [1]

'What are you doing at the moment?'

'Writing a book about Vesta Tilley.'

Some people now say, 'Who?' and the story goes a different
way: 'London's Idol', 'The Irving of the Halls', the highest-
earning woman in Britain in the 1880s; the woman who could
'fill any Hall anywhere'. Today, women who know the names
of obscure German philosophers and failed novelists do not
know who she was. If you want lasting fame, avoid popular
culture like the plague. Or, don't be working class and
successful.

'Why Vesta Tilley?' asks my questioner.

'Because I've always wanted to wear a tailcoat, and if I
can't wear one for the launch party of my own book about
Vesta Tilley then I never can.'

Downstairs my husband and daughter, who is twelve, are
singing. More precisely, she is singing and he is accompany-
ing her on the piano: the song they are busy with is one of
Vesta Tilley's greatest hits, 'Following in Father's Footsteps'.
This seems a complex irony to me, particularly as he is an
Anglican priest, and therefore still walks one of the few

remaining paths down which his daughter, categorically, cannot follow. She loves the song — along with a number of other Music Hall numbers which we have discovered since I started work on this book — and she sings it well, mocking him knowingly and enjoying the joke. Occasionally she will sing it when our friends come round in the evening: 'showing off' this is called nowadays, but she is also gracefully incorporating herself into our adult life. However, she has never suggested that she assume costume for it. Is this because in her jeans and T-shirt she does not feel the need, or because she, approaching adolescence and sensitive about her own gender identity and physical development, would find that alarming?

Last year was my daughter's final year in primary school; to celebrate the end of term and the departure to secondary school her class had a fancy dress party. In her form there was a girl who had committed herself entirely to being a tomboy; her name is Michela — she never wore anything but trousers and completely refused to act out her gender role; she would not even line up with the other girls on those ridiculous occasions when gender divisions were made, as they should not be at an ILEA primary school. Come the fancy dress party, considerable pressure was put on her, not, interestingly, so much by her peers with whom she got on well enough, but by the staff, to dress 'properly'. (An odd reversal this: it seems to me that she was allowed to deny her gender in daily life, but not at 'carnival'.) The same pressure was not apparently put on other children, because my daughter, who is of course my only informant on all of this, went happily as Super-Priest — a clear satire on the cult of the super-hero and on her own, rather ambivalent, social position as the vicar's kid in a working-class area. Michela, however, found a solution: she went dressed as Boy George. I was full of admiration for such sophistication and problem-solving ability; for such an elegant combination of flexibility and obstinacy. This does not, of course, probe the recesses of her mind: is she trying to gain power and privilege by aping the habit of her caste superiors? Is she buying herself out of sexual maturity by denying her 'femininity'? Or is she creating a freer place for herself by moving outside oppressive conventions? I see her now, a year later, coming and going from her all-girls' school, obliged to wear a uniform which identifies her gender to the world. She is approaching puberty; will the experience of living that childhood strengthen or weaken the woman she will become? She was not, is not, a camouflaged person, she was involved in an authority challenging gender-bending of her own. Of course she is not an exception; lots of small girls want to be boys (lots of big girls also) and it is important to note that none of the boys, inevitably, expressed their search for a freer space outside the limits imposed by authority by dressing as *women*. None the less, her deft handling of social pressure, her refusal to compromise, her complex challenge to the idea of dressing 'properly' at all, and the ebullience of her solution attract admiration, at least from her peers, and indeed from me.

But the story does raise questions: have we honestly — below the superficialities of clothes, which are of course not superficial at all — given this generation of young women, to whom my daughter belongs, any new space? Have we even chipped at the edges of the ideology of gender determination? Have we created new models, new images within popular culture, which our daughters can make use of in order to grow into New Women of a new sort? Can they begin to see gender identity as a choice they can make within a particular and specific social development? Have we set them free to be proud, not of who they are, but of whom they might be free to become? Or have we, once again, affirmed the power and superiority of men by suggesting that a woman's best route to individual power and freedom is to be 'like a man'?

Of course the 'tomboy' has been given special privileges within Western society: since Louisa M. Alcott's Jo, in *Little Women*, there have been a thousand books to tell us that the 'boyish' girl will grow into the most noble woman, free from the petty vanities and fiddly faults that are natural to the female state, and ideally grateful to the strong man who will tame her through love and give her femininity back to her as a gift. (Markedly less popular was Alcott's French contemporary, Madame Dieulafoy, an extraordinary transvestite, who 'always dressed as a man . . . but she maintained that a feminine education, that is to educate all children as girls was the only hope for the future'.[2]) It is partly to hide from ourselves the reality of children's sexuality that we let little girls play at being boys, and it is partly to train them in the knowledge of male excellence. Most of the 'gender-benders' of today have associated themselves with youth culture; there they can hide under the cover of childishness, 'a phase' they will be free to grow out of.

I turned to Vesta Tilley precisely because she too was a performer in popular culture. I wanted to use her as a way of looking again at Michela's story, and as a way of trying to find myself and my daughter's, and my friends' relationship to it.

I also wanted to write about Vesta Tilley because I have a weakness in that direction: I think she is terrific. Even the static and thinned-out version handed across sixty years, via shabby postcards and technically limited recordings, mediated through blurred memories and mediocre writing, beguiles me, pleases me. I am beguiled too by Amazon myths and the dreams of the warrior women; by the valiant and doomed Joan of Arc with her banner in her hand; by St Perpetua, whose stroppy boldness and personal authority still comes strongly across 1,650 years of pietist translations and Christian misrepresentation, and who took on maleness in her dreams and visions even as she breast-fed her son. I am enchanted by Virginia Woolf's *Orlando*, by Rose Macaulay's ungendered protagonist in *The Towers of Trebizond*, by the sinister power of Mademoiselle de Maupin in Théophile Gautier's novel of that name, by Annie Hall, by Greta Garbo in *Queen Christina*, by Marlene Dietrich, by the film *Sylvia Scarlett*, by Viola and Rosalind, and by the popular singer Annie Lennox. I longed to sail in Nancy's Amazon, rather than with the virtuous John in Swallow when I was still young enough to overlook the appalling class elitism of Arthur Ransome's books. I am even delighted, I have to confess, by the predominant street style of feminism: I did not become a feminist because we all look so wonderful, but I still think we do and I am pleased that we do.

I think this weakness for a certain sort of 'androgyny' in self-presentation by other women touches more people than just me. It is a pleasure mixed from so many ingredients: a nostalgia for an innocent and optimistic childhood, before we knew about the universal and lethal oppression of women, when we still thought we could make it; a place of escape from the competitiveness of femininity; a fear of a too blatant or aggressive sexuality; a delight that some women at least can mock maleness and society's penis-doting heterosexuality; a memory of magic, and a hope that one day gender won't be the determinant that it is; a recognition of how much we all really do owe to the lesbians of the past who kept the sexual options open and who chose male clothes as a symbol (however misguided, however unhappily) of that refusal to be made invisible.

But I began the last paragraph by saying it was a weakness, and I believe it is. Not because we should, on some puritanical, moralistic grounds be 'above' such things as style and clothes-consciousness. But because I am persuaded by my own arguments that, inevitably, in a historical reality where men and women are not equal, where gender is not just a determinant but also a prejudice, where men have power and have it (however this is analysed and described) at the expense of women, then women who use male-impersonation to gain for themselves, as individuals, money or fame or prestige or even physical space, are in fact affirming male superiority. The act of male-impersonation (whatever its radical intention or potential) is an act of collusion, of reaction. It is also an act of self-denial, of self-destruction.

Of course I believe it is important to play with ideas of appearance and expectation, of image and representation. I am

not a fiction writer for nothing. But male-impersonation —
within the theatrical conventions available — does not seek to
confuse; finally, it does not really require deception. It *pretends*
to be deceptive, and is thus, so to speak, doubly deceptive.

And yet . . . And yet using this dicey device Vesta Tilley
came a long way. The very last song she ever sang, at her
farewell performance in 1920, was 'Jolly Good Luck to the
Girl who Loves a Soldier'; when she reached the last chorus
and her clear voice sang out 'Girls, if you want to love a
soldier, you can all love ME', a stentorian voice from the
gallery called out 'We do!' The gender confusion is complete;
the British male is prepared to identify himself with 'the
girls'. Even so, women loved her too; the majority of her
greatest fans were women, who both courted her and named
their daughters after her.

Vesta Tilley — male-impersonator, singer, actress, Pantomime Principal Boy, silent-movie star and Member of
Parliament's wife — before whose be-trousered legs a queen of
England felt obliged to cover her face, still presents images
and provokes questions for twentieth-century women. The
greatest of the gender-benders. An extraordinary woman who
deserves a brassy book.

THE CURTAIN RAISER – VESTA TILLEY

In Worcester, in 1864, Vesta Tilley was born into working-class poverty; she never went to school and was employed full-time by the age of seven.

She died Lady de Frece, in 1952: widow of the Conservative MP Sir Walter de Frece, a resident of Monte Carlo, a rich and respected philanthropist.

And in between? In between she used all the resources she could command (except genital sexual performance) to break through or manipulate the barriers of class and gender which were so powerfully oppressive to working-class women in Victorian and Edwardian Britain. The great age of Music Hall spanned sixty years between 1860 and 1920. They were the years of her career: she was lucky, talented and determined.

Music Hall was born out of a curious mating between the industrialization – and hence urbanization – of the British working class and the preposterous laws that governed theatrical performances in the first half of the nineteenth century. Until 1845 only Drury Lane, Covent Garden and the Theatres Royal could present proper plays; elsewhere 'wholly spoken theatrical activity for gain' was expressly forbidden. To avoid breaking these laws, other theatres were obliged to add elements of music or circus to all productions. At the same time, taverns and drinking houses throughout the country were providing amateur sing-songs to accompany the business of drinking. These tavern concerts and glee-clubs flourished happily in the eighteenth and early nineteenth

centuries, ranging comfortably from the vulgar to the aristo-
cratic. As Prince of Wales, George IV sang bawdy drinking
songs 'with considerable taste and humour' along with
Sheridan, the playwright, Beau Brummel, the dandy, and
Sydney Smith, the clergyman, at the Neapolitan Club in
London. But by the 1840s such activities had fallen into
disrepute, along with drinking itself.

A few of the 'new' Halls of the 1850s found some support
from the establishment, as *The Times* in 1856 suggests:

The Canterbury Hall is . . . one of a class of establishments
affording the means of recreation for the respectable classes far above
the entertainment proffered a few years since at establishments of
this kind.[1]

But by and large the view was that Music Hall audiences were
'mixed crowds of folly and vice' and it was legitimate to
wonder 'whether the Music Hall was the place for gentlemen
to go, or even for a greengrocer, a chimney-sweep or
costermonger or any man who entertained a liking to be
thought respectable.'[2] While Henry Mayhew, no moralistic
puritan, found his visit to a Penny Gaff (the socially lowest
form of Variety Hall) in the 1850s 'perfect in its wickedness
. . . ingenuity has been exerted to its uttermost lest an
obscene thought should be passed by', he lamented that the
performance was 'forcing into the brains of the childish
audience thoughts that must embitter a lifetime and descend
from father to child like some bodily infirmity.'[3]

And yet, in less than fifty years the first Royal Command
Variety Performance was presented by Oswald Stoll, assisted
by Walter de Frece and Alfred Butt (all three soon to have
the dignity of knighthoods conferred upon them). Conan
Doyle, neglecting his great detective for the evening, wrote
for the *Era*:

To what a beautiful and lordly pleasure house the King and Queen
came! For richness of colour, for tactefulness of arrangement and for
real prettiness the general effect would be difficult to excel, and it is
wonderfully chaste and artistic.[4]

The Times was even more explicit:

Last night the art of variety theatre received a new and single honour — an honour too which the art has earned by its steady progress from obscurity (not unmixed with obscenity) to general favour. . . . The scene to which they [the Royal Household] lent their distinction must have convinced them that vulgar display is by no means a characteristic of the modern music hall.[5]

Of course this move towards respectability was bought at a price: possibly the price was Music Hall itself. The concerted efforts, particularly of the great magnates of the Hall syndicates, to raise the tone of Music Hall and attract richer customers stole the form from the working classes, where it had its roots and its meaning, and in doing so destroyed the goose which laid their golden eggs. The point here is not to argue whether the upward mobility of Music Hall was a good or bad thing, but to record it as an extraordinary phenomenon, given the common myths of class stability and prudishness in Victorian society.

And Vesta Tilley, who was one of the 'turns' at that Royal Command Performance of 1912, rose on that same swing of social change. The first professional woman performer on the Halls, a Miss Ellen Caulfield, appeared in 1860, only eight years before Vesta Tilley turned professional. At that time even the stage was scandalous; the Halls were certainly no place for a lady. Vesta Tilley came from a background of dingy if not sordid poverty. Moreover, she established her fame with an act that in Victorian terms ran every risk of being seen as obscene; both because she mimicked and mocked the state of maleness, and because in order to do so she had to reveal an indecent amount of herself, to a society which still felt that the 'sight of stocking was something shocking'.

None the less, using this risky performance in a despised medium, she rose to a social eminence that permitted her to be presented at Court in 1923; the *Evening News* recorded the occasion without so much as mentioning her stage name or fame:

The jewelled gowns which were the feature of the court this year will be long remembered . . . One of the loveliest was the *toilette* designed by Mr Reville for Lady de Frece.[6]

Although by then her husband was a Deputy Lieutenant for the county of Lancashire, a knight and a Member of Parliament, it is worth noting that Vesta Tilley did not achieve her class 'escape' through marriage — though other Music Hall stars did, most notably Connie Gilchrist who became Countess of Orkney, and Belle Bilton who married Lord Dunlo in a splendid scandal of the 1890s. Walter de Frece came from a Jewish family, only slightly more prosperous than Vesta Tilley's own, and like her he made both his money and his reputation in the Music Halls.

The nineteenth century was not a good time for working-class women. What Vesta Tilley pulled off was a remarkable achievement, which she both enjoyed and paid for. It is worth examining.

Vesta Tilley was born Matilda Powles on 13 May 1864 in Commandery Street, Worcester. On her baptismal certificate her father, Henry Powles, is described as a china painter. About her mother nothing is known; Vesta Tilley mentions her only once, in a minor anecdote, in her autobiography *Recollections of Vesta Tilley*. She did, however, have thirteen children, of whom Matilda was the second. Vesta Tilley never mentioned her brothers and sisters either, although in her will she left £10,000 to each of them.

Her family sentiment was reserved for her father, to whom she was completely devoted. Part of this devotion must have sprung from her curious upbringing, but since she was neither the oldest child nor the long-awaited son, the upbringing itself must have been a consequence of some early affinity or special relationship. Harry Powles was an enterprising extrovert. He was a considerable musician — both playing and composing. For a while he had a semi-pro act,

'Harry Ball, Tramp Musician and his incredible performing Dog' (Fatso, the family pet, trained in a few basic tricks). But in 1867, as the Music Halls began their wave of expansion, he took a job as Chairman of the newly opened Theatre Royal in Gloucester. The Music Hall Chairman acted as a master of ceremonies, ruling not from the stage, but from the front table of the House. Halls at the beginning did not have stalls, but a ground floor of tables, and the consumption of alcohol and food was as important as the acts themselves. His task was not only to introduce the acts – the exaggerated and verbose gusto which became customary for this role is rightly famous – but also to control the audience, encourage the purchase of drinks, engage in repartee with both performers and audience and get unpopular acts off the stage as quickly as possible. (The Chairman's role was destroyed in the mid-1880s by the introduction of stalls and proscenium arches; it was then possible to bring the curtain down on any act that was not well-received, and the power shifted to the stage manager. Moreover, the introduction of electrical boards to announce the number of the act, and the increasing literacy of the audience – which enabled them to buy and use programmes – meant that the Chairman was left without a job and gently disappeared.)

Chairmen in the early and rowdy days of the Halls had to be forceful and flamboyant characters. The famous Baron Courtney in London, for example, dripped diamonds and other jewellery from his costume; once, when he dropped a ring, he reassured the anxious spectator searching for it that it really didn't matter because he had plenty more at home. Not only did this casual glamour have an obvious appeal to the generally poor audience, it must also have compensated for, or balanced, the autocracy with which the Chairman was obliged to fulfil his role. It says a great deal about Harry Powles's personality that, despite his performing and composing talents, it was as a Chairman that he found his professional *métier*. At about this time he adopted his stage name Harry Ball, and became known by it exclusively.

His daughter got her first introduction to theatrical life in Gloucester, when her father began to take her to rehearsals. As any child might, she enjoyed these immensely and quickly developed a musical ear, singing the songs she heard with her father at home. Like many extroverted men, Harry Ball obviously felt that her performances reflected credit on him and he lost no opportunity of showing her off to his friends; as she preferred his songs and his accompaniments to all others, it must have been a delightful ego-trip for them both. From parlour singing, Matilda quickly progressed to her first public performance. In 1868 her father was offered a new job, as Chairman and manager of St George's Music Hall in Nottingham – like many others it had opened in the 1850s as a gin-palace and dance-hall and was now turning to live Music Hall. Before leaving Gloucester, Harry Ball was given the customary farewell benefit, and to this naturally sympathetic audience he introduced his daughter, now four years old. Like most stage-parents he dressed her to emphasize her youth, in a little white skirt and Red-Riding-Hood cape. The paternal advice was brief and to the point: carrying her on to the stage himself, he set her down amid the all-male and probably drunken audience and said, 'Now don't be frightened. Sing as if you mean it. Do not cough. Speak up.' Not surprisingly, she went down a bomb with the crowd. After her song she had a brief moment of hesitation:

I stood there, uncertain for the first time what to do, because he had not told me which way to leave the stage. He came to my rescue. He walked on and picked me up, hugging me with pride and delight, and carried me off to more applause.[7]

Once in Nottingham, not surprisingly, there was no stopping her, nor apparently him. Despite the insalubrious surroundings and the very late hours, her father wrote some songs especially for her and allowed her to perform regularly under the billing of 'The Great Little Tilley'. Although it was not uncommon for quite small children to perform on the Halls at this time, it was unusual to find child soloists (as opposed to those like Charlie Chaplin, Stan Laurel, Dan Leno and Little Tich who all worked in troupes with their families) and certainly to find ones as young as Vesta Tilley; but from the age of about five she was under continual pressure to perform.

The explosion of Music Halls had led to an escalating need to import talent from outside the immediate locality. The Great Little Tilley's charming act became known further afield and she was invited to perform in Halls in Derby, Dudley, Leicester and other towns. Initially her father, who had his job and family to consider, reckoned it was impossible for him to tour with her and found a 'kindly and obliging neighbour woman' to accompany her. It cannot have been an easy life, travelling in discomfort, and giving continual performances. In these early days 'turns' were very much longer than they later became — seldom shorter than forty-five minutes. Performers were expected to change their acts regularly, so that they had to learn a lot of new material and rehearse it privately as well as rehearse with a different band at each new Hall. Victorian lodging-houses were probably not the ideal haven for small children, even if accompanied by the most obliging and kindly of neighbours.

These pressures, plus her rapidly growing success, led in 1872 to a major change in the family's life. Harry Ball resigned his position and became instead her personal manager. To compensate presumably for his loss of earnings he refurbished his old act and offered managements two separate acts at once. From then on, Vesta Tilley and her father were on the road together for about six months of every year, mostly in the Midlands, but gradually further afield, leaving her mother and the rest of the children in Nottingham.

In her *Recollections* Vesta Tilley records that from this point onwards she became completely absorbed in her professional life. Although from 1870 primary education was compulsory, the law was not strictly observed, and although she did some lessons when she was at home, and also helped her mother in

the house, the principal focus was on practising and performing. She had little else: after introducing her to the rather
questionable and unhealthy life of an itinerant Variety artiste,
her adored and controlling father did almost everything
possible to protect her from the moral and social consequences of that choice. Circumstances and indeed her father
made it impossible for her to form other emotional bonds —
she seems to have been allowed few real friendships and even
when she was grown-up her father forbade her much social
contact with her contemporaries.

After a few years the precocious Matilda began to feel that
there were limitations to the sweet-little-girl act:

Young as I was, I had in song run through the whole gamut of
female characters from baby songs to old maids' ditties and I
concluded that female costume was rather a drag [sic!]. I felt I would
express myself better if I were dressed as a boy.[8]

She herself tells a charming story about how she came to
assume male-impersonation as a part of her act. The *Recollections* are full of inaccuracies and even untruths — Vesta Tilley
throughout her life told innumerable and contradictory anecdotes about herself, offering different explanations for the
same facts, even about how she chose her stage name and the
inspiration for her most famous songs, so there is no
particular reason to believe this story; rather, it reflects how
she wished to think of her childhood and her father. She
relates that after having supper and kissing her father good
night she was on her way to bed when she saw his coat and
hat hanging as usual on their hook. She sneaked them
upstairs and tried them on — though the coat trailed and she
had to stuff the hat with paper to make it stay on the top of
her head. Thus dressed, and feeling both shocked and
excited, she began to imitate in front of a mirror, the male
singers she had seen on the Halls. She was so deeply
immersed in her own performance that she was not aware of
her father's eyes upon her. After a while he spoke, and she was
both startled and guilty. But he congratulated her on the act

and asked if she would like to have proper men's clothes for a number in her performance. Relieved at his forgiveness and excited at the idea, she agreed eagerly.

He had a small evening suit made for her: tails and white tie 'no larger than would fit an ordinary rabbit'.[9] He decided that the best way to introduce male-impersonation into her act was through mimicry: he looked to the extremely popular tenor, Sim Reeves, then at the height of his fame and touring the Midlands. He had an instantly recognizable large black moustache, which made a caricature simple, and a repertoire of well-known songs including such Victorian sentimental classics as 'Anchors Aweigh' and 'Come into the Garden Maud'. This latter, originally composed for him using Tennyson's lyrics (though not to the great poet's satisfaction) by Michael William Balfe in 1857, became perhaps the best-known of all the Victorian parlour songs. It was the first song that Vesta Tilley sang as a male-impersonator.

In 1872 Vesta Tilley made her first appearance as a male-impersonator at Day's Concert Hall in Birmingham. At the beginning of the 1870s it was perhaps the finest and most prestigious Music Hall in the provinces, at a time when, with the emergence of the star system, the eating and drinking elements of Music Hall were becoming secondary to the business of performance. She was billed as 'The Great Little Tilley, the Pocket Sim Reeves', and she was an instant hit — witnessed by the fact that she was paid the then princely sum of £5 a week. After this engagement her career began to take off seriously. She started to obtain higher billings, to earn ever-higher salaries (up to £12 a week before she was ten) and to 'pack the Halls'.

Gradually she dropped her earlier repertoire and concentrated solely on male-impersonation, adding original material to the imitations and beginning to develop her art of character creation. Women, who were now beginning to attend Music Hall, found the little girl touching, and encouraged her to develop highly sentimental 'tear-jerkers' of which 'Poor Joe' (also called 'Near the Workhouse Door'), in which she acted the part of a scruffy orphan boy 'moved along' by an unsympathetic policeman, was perhaps her greatest hit, and drew tears from the audience. Other early songs, however, were of a more brassy nature: love songs, obviously given an edge sung by a female child in full adult male dress, had titles like 'Strolling along with Nancy' and 'Rosie May' and were written especially for her, mainly by her father. And as a hint of the great dandy songs to come, another early success was 'The Pet of Rotten Row' (Rotten Row was still the great promenade and riding centre of fashionable London in the 1870s).

With her mounting success her father found it less and less necessary to perform himself and from the time Vesta Tilley was about ten she had become the sole financial support of the rapidly growing family. He became instead her full-time manager, her principal song-writer, her only confidant and her chaperone in the cut-throat world of the emerging provincial Music Hall tour. Obviously they managed to return home to Nottingham periodically because the Powles produced a further seven children in the years after father and daughter left home — but these diversions from professionalism and from being the centre of her father's attention were never mentioned in later life by his daughter. They toured more and more widely, serving a vigorous apprenticeship and making useful contacts. In Edinburgh they became friendly with Edward Moss, who was to become one of the greatest and most successful of the Music Hall impresarios and syndicators, founding the great Moss empire circuit. He was to pioneer the concept of the 'palatial' Hall, built as a theatre not a drinking place, which made him and others extremely rich in the 1890s and 1900s.

Vesta Tilley also became acquainted with Henry de Frece, first in his Gaiety Hall in Sheffield, and later in his Hall of the same name in Liverpool; and with Mrs Stoll who ran a successful small Hall in Manchester. Her son, Oswald Stoll, with Edward Moss and Henry de Frece's son Walter, later developed the respectable Music Hall, attractive to the middle and upper classes around the turn of the century. Harry Ball was much impressed by the ambition of these Hall owners, and pursued both professional and personal connections with them which affected Vesta Tilley's career, and indeed, her whole life.

Inevitably they met up with other touring performers, although the itinerant life-style made it difficult to form real or long-lasting relationships. One Christmas — when the Hall artistes had to perform three, instead of the usual one or two, daily shows — they shared lodgings with Dan Leno and his family. He was to become probably the greatest Music Hall comedian but at this point, only a couple of years older than Vesta Tilley, he was acting in his family acrobatic show and specializing in clog-dancing. Dan Leno seems to have been one of the few friendships from this time which endured, and later, when they were both married, they went on holiday together with their respective spouses. It is typical of Vesta Tilley that she should describe their friendship and happiness in considerable detail in her memoirs, but fail to record both the extraordinary distinction to which he rose and the painful account of his extremely public collapse into insanity and early death. The latter was understandably difficult for her: even contemporary accounts agreed that the cause of his collapse was the strain of appearing so constantly on stage from such an early age — but he was three years older than Vesta Tilley had been when he started performing, he did not go solo until his teens and was at the time of his death only forty-three.

It was this childhood friend who was to describe London as 'a large village on the Thames where the principal industries are Music Hall and the confidence trick'.[10] In the twelve years between Vesta Tilley's birth and her first appearance in London, Music Halls blossomed and flourished to an extraordinary degree. As early as 1866, the Select Committee on Theatrical Licences and Regulations recorded that since 1851 thirty-two new Music Halls had been built, not including 'a large number of small tavern concert halls', which could accommodate 50,000 people nightly, at an investment of over £500,000. Of these Halls at least ten were West End theatres, led by the Alhambra in Leicester Square. Already the upward mobility of Music Hall was beginning, and it was drifting away from its origins in the East End and south of the river.

This shift was helped enormously by the rapidly improving system of public transport. The growth of suburban commuterism refocused the West End as the centre of popular middle-class entertainment, and the theatres and Music Halls there were able to anticipate a more than purely local audience. This permitted longer runs for individual performers and accelerated the move away from amateurism and a drinking community. The West End Halls, because their audiences were irregular and transient, encouraged professionalism and a more limited repertoire, consisting of only the best-known 'hit' songs. This policy led to a reluctance to introduce new material and, by 1900, to much shorter 'turns'. Many commentators including Vesta Tilley herself came to believe that this was one of the principal causes of the decline in Music Hall in the twentieth century.

Not surprisingly, Harry Ball began to want his daughter to appear in London. This was not, initially, for the money. With the exception of the very great stars, who pulled fabulous salaries from the beginning (Leotard, the French aerealist and the original 'daring young man on the flying trapeze, who flew through the air with the greatest of ease', as another Music Hall star George Leybourne had sung of him, made £180 a week for his 1868 season) performers were paid less in London than in the provinces, presumably because there was more competition. It was, for the Powles, more a question of fame, prestige and long-term investment. An artiste who was a success in London could hope to work towards real star status; and increasingly the wages and spin-offs – the postcard trade, the endorsement of songs, and roles in Pantomime – were developing a cult of stardom.

When Vesta Tilley was first offered work in London both she and her father were appalled to discover that she would only be paid £3 a week. But they quickly learned that all London performers appeared in more than one show at a time. The gross inadequacy of changing rooms in the Music Halls scarcely mattered because everyone was performing at two, three, or even four Halls a night, with wild dashes by hired brougham in between. In London the 'twice-nightly show', which demonstrated the change from 'Variety entertainment while drinking' to 'the show's the thing', did not become the practice until well into the 1900s. In the 1870s, Music Hall shows were immensely long, consisting of up to thirty turns — of which the most popular might last up to an hour. This made the cross-city sprints possible, but must still have required elaborate organization and cooperation between performers and rival managements. In 1906, for example, when, admittedly, turns had become shorter, Whit Cunliffe, a popular tenor, appeared in one week at the Chelsea Palace at 7.10 p.m. and 9.45 p.m.; at the Euston, in King's Cross, at 7.45 p.m. and 10.40 p.m.; and at the Oxford, Oxford Street, at 8.50 p.m.

By then, of course, things were rather better organized than when Vesta Tilley and her father first arrived in London in 1874, but already the impossible schedules had become a popular joke. Bessie Bellwood, who was the first great woman star, 'the Queen of the Halls' — overshadowed in memory by Marie Lloyd, but in her day unrivalled for broad humour, swift repartee and a string of powerful cockney songs — had a highly popular number, 'The Pro's Coachman', with the chorus:

First he's at the Tivoli,
Then he's at the Pav. [London Pavilion]
Then he comes out, and begins to shout
'Fifteen minutes you have,
So drive like hell to the Paragon.'[11]

The Powles took the plunge. They hired lodgings in Kennington, a carriage for the transport and an agent to make sense of the bookings. Still billed as 'The Great Little Tilley',

Matilda started performing nightly at the Canterbury in Lambeth, Lusby's in Mile End and the Marylebone, each at £3 a week. With new expenses they initially found that they could not make ends meet, but before long she was making £5 per show per week and they were able to manage.

Very shortly the question of her stage name was raised. Not only was 'The Great Little Tilley' too long and cumbersome for the London style but, more importantly, the customers were expressing genuine confusion as to whether she was really a boy or a girl. Male (and for that matter female) impersonation depends for its effect largely on the knowledge of the audience that it is an impersonation. (I once went to see Hinge and Brackett with someone who failed to grasp that this was a drag act − God knows how − and was therefore completely baffled and bored. This was instructive, although from his point of view not much fun.)

Edward Villiers, the manager of the Canterbury, one of the leading Halls, became aware of the problem and asked the Powles to change Matilda's stage name. There are a number of stories, some of them directly put about by Vesta Tilley, as to how they chose the name Vesta: (after the brand of matches, 'a bright spark', is one of the more popular versions). In the *Recollections* she says that her father chose a few two-syllable names from the dictionary and she picked one out of a hat. After this, from here on she became Vesta Tilley, absolutely. She was formally addressed (which meant by the press as well, who never used first names) as Miss Tilley − until she retired and became Lady de Frece (she never seems to have used Mrs de Frece). Her personal friends, her father, and her husband, all called her Vesta. One more link with her childhood was broken.

After she had become established in London, Vesta Tilley set a work pattern which was unbroken until her father died in 1889. She lodged and worked in London for about three months of every year, and she toured the provinces for about six. The remaining three months were increasingly filled by her rising success as a Pantomime Principal Boy.

The traditions of Pantomime are ancient and complex, but by the 1860s it had established itself securely as a respectable and traditional comedy performance: the only kind of theatre middle-class women and children could attend. Augustus Harris, the director of Drury Lane, one of the ancient Royal Charter theatres, presented a Pantomime every season, and he specialized increasingly in extremely elaborate stage settings. In one production of *Beauty and the Beast* he had a ship so large than tram lines had to be laid down to get it on and off stage; in his *Sinbad*,* a mechanical bird representing the story's traditional giant roc occupied the entire stage for one scene and was meant to lift into the air, carrying Sinbad (actually it broke down and stuck, and the curtain had to be brought down for over an hour while the stage-hands smashed the poor bird with hammers). Even without such mishaps, scene changes, of which there were many, could take up to fifteen minutes. In order to fill the gap Harris, and others, conceived the idea of having characters appear 'front cloth' — in front of the curtain. Since the performers best able to fill in were the Music Hall stars, they were increasingly employed in Pantomime and allowed to perform their own Variety material.

This innovation, although it proved quickly popular with audiences, was ill-received by the critics. Dickens in his history of Pantomime wrote:

Then came the deluge, the floodgates of Music Hall were opened and everything that was agreeable about the 'good comic pantomime' was drained out.[12]

---

* Until well after the First World War 'Sinbad' was spelled 'Sinbadd'; Pantomime titles were not the simple folk-story names, but extremely long and punning jokes. Once when Vesta Tilley was appearing in 'Aladdin' it was billed 'A LAD IN whom we have inVESTAd our hopes unTILL 'E has to leave us.' For simplicity's sake I have referred to all Pantomimes by their contemporary names.

In a *Times* article of 1881 middle-class disapproval of Music Hall was undisguised:

We may say of the present day pantomime that the trail of the Music Hall is all over it. I admit to the extreme ability of certain music hall comedians. I object however, altogether, to the intrusion of such artistes into the domain of Pantomime, and I say so because they, and others not so able, bring with them so to speak an atmosphere which it is sad to see imported into the theatre. They bring with them not only their songs, which when offensive in their wording are sometimes made doubly dangerous by their tunefulness, not only their dances, which are usually vulgar when they are not inane, but their style and manners and 'gags' which are generally the most deplorable of all. The objection to Music Hall artists on the stage . . . is that they have the effect of familiarising audiences and children especially, with a style and a kind of singing, dancing and 'business' which however it may be relished by a certain class of the population, ought steadily to be confined to its original habitat.[13]

Other writers complained as strenuously about the 'infinitesimally clothed damsels', and the vulgarity of opulence — 'pantomimes have become all legs and lighting'.

But however much they objected, the innovation had come to stay, and for Music Hall artistes it was a welcome one: it could give them up to three or four months of steady work when they did not have to be on the road; it gave them the opportunity to develop sustained characterization, and a chance to work with other performers. It also, significantly, gave middle-class audiences a chance to sample Music Hall performance in a safe context which proved important for the development of the form. The hallowed antiquity of Pantomime seems to have taken some of the moral danger out of cross-dressing on the stage. Vesta Tilley was only one of the Music Hall performers who was able to use this shift in public appreciation to her own advantage. She played her first Principal Boy in Portsmouth in 1877 and thereafter played Pantomime every winter for the next fifteen years.

In 1882, as a mark of her rapid rise to fame, she was

invited to perform at Drury Lane in a Harris production of Sinbad. Her father had initially refused to let her appear as anything except Principal Boy — for which role the greatest female star of the early eighties, Nellie Power ('a serio-comic who sang "The Boy I Love is up in the Gallery" in such a way that every single boy in the gallery hoped, no, believed, that it was he')[14] had already been booked. However, Harris agreed to write a special role for her and allow her to sing any material of her own choosing: so she appeared as Captain Tralala, the first 'Second Boy', now usual in Pantomime.

Drury Lane represented the pinnacle of popular Panto-mime, but Vesta Tilley only appeared there once again. She fell out with Harris, who booked her to be Principal Boy in *Dick Whittington* (always her favourite) for the 1890 season. When the time came, however, he decided to exploit a current society scandal in order to create a stage sensation. Belle Bilton, who with her sister Flo had sung the Halls, secretly married Lord Dunlo, heir to the Earl of Clancarty. The groom's parents, properly scandalized, packed him off to Australia only nine days after the wedding, and on his return persuaded him to sue for divorce on the grounds of her adultery. Unfortunately for Papa, the young man broke down in the middle of the trial and in court passionately declared his complete conviction of Belle's innocence. Harris saw his chance, and decided to play *Beauty and the Beast* instead. He announced that Lady Dunlo would play Beauty — tastefully hinting at the scandal of her husband's 'change of face'. By 1890 Vesta Tilley played second fiddle to no one, but was bound by her contract. When she discovered that she was expected to appear in all except the first act and the last number with an enormous 'Beast' mask over her head, rendering all singing and character acting impossible, she was outraged. She insisted that the masked scenes be played by a stand in, while she hopped out of the theatre every night to sing a Music Hall turn at the Variety next door, thus doubling her salary. She 'never quite forgave Harris' and never performed for him again.

Her anger went deep. Curiously, in her *Recollections* she never mentions the scandal attached to Belle Bilton and the production, complaining only of the compulsory substitution of *Beauty and the Beast* for *Dick Whittington*. She was already becoming the 'good girl' of the Halls, the nice one a boy could take home to mother. She always and deliberately distanced herself from the sexual vitality that Music Hall was introducing into middle-class society. By the 1890s she had already thrown in her lot with the 'respectables' − Oswald Stoll, who was at one stage in love with her, Edward Moss and the de Freces who, for reasons of profit and social advancement, wanted to create a 'high-class Variety', free from all taint of vulgarity. Although Stoll did not open the Coliseum − the dream of 'respectable' Music Hall, a palace fit for the reception of royalty − until 1904, the gap between the two factions was already vast: those who felt that Music Hall came from and fundamentally belonged to the working class, who enjoyed the bawdy element and conspicuously indulged in the new freedom that their success and money gave them; and those, like Vesta Tilley, who wanted upward mobility and were prepared to pay for it. She did not want to be involved in a performance where the main draw was not her talent, but a social scandal based on the sexual attraction and class ambition of another, and admittedly mediocre, performer. She took herself and her work very seriously.

Indeed Vesta Tilley's seriousness about 'her art' emerged most visibly in Pantomime, which added a depth and range to her acting abilities. Right from the start at the age of thirteen, she set certain ground rules with a remarkable stubbornness. Contrary to normal practice, she insisted that all her roles carried at least one 'straight scene', a moment of pathos seriously presented, and into which no comedy was allowed to intrude. This idea of playing one scene for some emotional depth gradually took off in Pantomime (although now it is usually played by the heroine), but she was the first to demand it and it became immensely popular. Willson Disher, who saw her perform, was of the opinion that she might have changed our idea of the Principal Boy entirely if she had had a mind to, but she was too good a trouper to upset its frolics. In all other scenes of the fairy-tale she obeyed the rules.[15]

From 1874, when she came to London, until 1888, her life maintained a relentless momentum of performance, travel and rehearsal. She relates that in 1881 in Dublin she formed a brief relationship with an American actor, whom she fancied because 'he looked just like my father and loved his mother'.[16] Although she went to the dock to see him off when he returned to America, she had no trouble in turning down his offer of marriage. She could not leave either her father or her work.

In 1888, however, she met a young man who won her father's explicit approval. Very wisely this young man courted her almost entirely through her father, who unbent so far as to let his twenty-four-year-old daughter go to her first-ever dance with him.

Walter de Frece was the eldest son of Henry de Frece who had once been the proprietor of the Worcester Alhambra; in the late 1870s he had started to develop one of the first chains of Music Halls, linked in the public mind because each house was called 'The Gaiety'. He obviously hoped for better things socially for his son than mere Music Hall; Walter had been educated at the Liverpool Institute and then in Brussels (not only were the sons of Music Hall entrepreneurs not welcome at British public schools, but the de Freces were also Jewish and therefore the social prejudice against them was considerable). In 1888, Walter, just turned twenty, was apprenticed to a Liverpool architect, but he was passionately committed to a theatrical career. He was exactly the sort of character that Vesta Tilley most often represented: the masher, or dandy, the young-man-about-town. He had a reputation as the best-dressed man in Liverpool and his lifelong friend Oswald Stoll recalled in Walter's obituary in 1935 that 'he was a noted dandy and when he took money at the pay-box he refused to touch it with bare hands, insisting on wearing gloves; but he was an extremely humourous man'.[17]

Throughout 1888−9 the couple wrote to each other; in addition Walter came nearly every weekend to visit her wherever she was playing. This must have been Vesta Tilley's first experience of any regular, sustained relationship, except with her father.

This friendship, already important, soon became crucial because in 1889, while she was playing at a small Hall in South Shields, her father contracted enteric fever and died very suddenly. He was only forty-seven. With his death Vesta Tilley lost not only her father, but her manager, the principal composer of her material, the only close friend that she had, and the man who had controlled her professional and personal life absolutely for over twenty years. The whole responsibility for maintaining her mother and the younger children also fell on her shoulders.

She and Walter de Frece became engaged almost immediately. He wanted to marry at once, but she insisted that he complete his training. However, in August 1890 he broke his apprenticeship articles, quarrelled with his father and appeared in London, insisting that they marry at once. Vesta Tilley crumpled immediately and on 16 August 1890 they were married at Brixton Registry Office by special licence. Walter made a considerable mess of all the arrangements: initially he applied for the licence to the Lambeth Burial Board, who directed him to the workhouse; he was late for the wedding, having overslept; he had forgotten to order a hackney cab and arrived in a shabby cart, and when he climbed down his hat blew away in the wind. All of this must have delighted Vesta Tilley as it was exactly the sort of incident she frequently presented on stage. But the incompetence, unless a highly elaborate psychological reading is taken, must be put down to the exuberance of young love: Walter de Frece was a highly efficient and intelligent young man, whose entrepreneurial skill and imaginative zest served the couple well.

It was an extremely convenient marriage for Vesta Tilley, and it was also a remarkably happy and strong one. They seem to have been very well-suited and to have assisted each other professionally and personally for the next forty-five years. Walter became a general theatrical entrepreneur: he built and owned a chain of Halls, all called The Hippodrome; he set up various travelling companies; and after 1912 became increasingly involved in Conservative Party politics. But, as Stoll also remarks in the obituary, 'Most of his life was spent in managing the affairs of Vesta Tilley, and no artistic affairs have ever been managed better.'[18]

This was not the usual hyperbole of the obituary writer. After her marriage Vesta Tilley developed not just in fame, which might have happened anyway, but as a performer. Later we will look at the precise content of her act in the 1890s and 1900s, but the change is important. Willson Disher indicates what happened:

Some of her songs in the eighties hardly bear the imprint of her personality at all. Some are the kind that any red-nosed comic or serio-comic might have sung. It was after she had become the London Idol, with full assurance of the public's loyalty, that she gave us something more than entertainment – something that has direct bearing on life.

At the beginning of the nineties she was still singing the praises of those who were 'ready and right for a row or a fight', but a little later came 'Algy – The Pic—cad—illy John—ny with the little glass eye'. He was as rollicking as his forerunners right until the last line of the last verse when you heard that behind his back the girls thought him a 'jay'. Then there arrived the young man called Brown who went to Paris for the weekend with a 'fair demoiselle' who turned out to be his own wife. Once again you see Vesta Tilley was telling the story against the masher she mimicked.

Henceforth instead of merging her own personality into that of the character she acted, she brought her wits to bear on him critically. By pretending to be young men for so long, she had come to understand them better than they did themselves. That is why we had to see them, ourselves, not as we could see them in real life, but as they were when they were viewed through a clever woman's eyes.[19]

Disher sees this new confidence growing out of her assurance of the audiences' love; but it corresponds very closely in time with the loss of her father and her marriage to Walter de Frece. Walter does not seem to have been a particularly dominating personality, indeed he adored her and they seem to have operated with considerable personal equality. She did not just go on working, her work radically improved: perhaps she was unconsciously wise not to choose a husband either older or from a higher class than herself who would have had difficulty in tolerating a wife on the Halls. I think she fell in love with the thing that she mimicked; and that gave her a freedom and authority which showed in her creative work.

Walter encouraged her to develop, artistically and also professionally. Although the Music Hall remained both the basis of her fame and the ideal medium for her performance, Vesta Tilley went on in the next years to play burlesque and straight theatre; she also recorded songs, developed her promotional potential, made films and, perhaps most importantly, she conquered America.

She returned to her usual work immediately after the marriage, which the couple tried unsuccessfully to keep secret: at her first performance she was greeted with the Wedding March and a standing ovation. Almost immediately, however, she collapsed and was obliged to stop work entirely for eighteen months. Given the discretion of the news media at the time and the fact that Vesta Tilley herself gives no clues whatsoever, it is impossible to know what her illness was. It was certainly serious: she was in hospital for nearly nine months and treated on a medical innovation of the time, a water bed. At one point her condition was sufficiently critical for her doctor to issue daily bulletins and for one evening newspaper to announce her death as its frontpage story. Thereafter, despite the fact that she continued her gruelling schedule for nine months of the year, her 'frail health' was offered as the reason why she and Walter de Frece had to spend three months of every winter in the South of France. Apart from this annual holiday, she demonstrated no other signs of debility the rest of the year. Walter de Frece's devotion to her comfort may have made it possible for her to 'catch up' on all the holidays she had never had.

So it was not only professionally that she gained from the marriage: she was also now permitted to be the more traditional Victorian middle-class woman, delicately laid on a sofa, treated as fragile. She gained a chance to relax, to take holidays and importantly to settle into a proper home.

The single most important consequence of her marriage, however, was the chance to work in America; a chance she took as soon as she had recovered from her illness.

America. And American Vaudeville.
Vaudeville was America in motley, the national relaxation. To the Palace, the Colonial, the Alhambra, the Orpheum, the Keith Circuit and chain variety houses, New York to Los Angeles we flocked, vicariously to don the false nose, let down our back hair and forget. Vaudeville was the threatre of the people, its brassy assurance a dig in the Nation's ribs, its simplicity as naive as the Circus.[20]

American Vaudeville and British Music Hall are often treated as though they were the same phenomenon. They shared some stars, and the theatres in which they were presented looked, by the 1890s, rather similar, but they were very different animals, with different histories and different expectations.

Vaudeville, in its full-grown form, was an entertainment of the American lower-middle class; a class larger and more important in America than in Britain. It was never so extensively patronized either by the 'bloods', the worldly young aristocrats who found it provincial, nor by the urban poor who found it too expensive and too proper. In America, long before England, Variety Entertainment divided itself rigorously between 'smutty' burlesque and 'clean' Vaudeville. As Douglas Gilbert put it:

Burlesque, in which the height of humour centred about the apertures of the human body, wandered to the Tenderloins leaving [Vaudeville] to work Main Street and Broadway.[21]

From early days, then, the gap which British Music Hall filled with its own speciality – 'innuendo' – did not exist in America. England's most popular Music Hall comedienne Marie Lloyd, for instance, failed there, not because her work was too smutty but because no one could understand that it was smutty at all; and having heard of her as the 'bluest' female in British Music Hall they simply did not have a tradition by which to understand what she was up to – the singing of 'innocent songs' in a style that made them precisely as 'sexual' as each individual member of the audience wanted to cope with.

Vaudeville was also much more professional – it relied less on the building, the atmosphere, the garish splendour that the English working class wanted, and far more on the excellence of performance. This was partly geographical: the big cities in America tended to be further apart and between them lay vast spaces that were scarcely economic from the theatrical point of view. It was therefore more convenient to tour Variety Shows, complete with their own managers and orchestras, through a series of one-night stands, in towns which did not boast a purpose-built regular theatre or Music Hall, and which lacked the amenities for eating, promenading and drinking which were integral to British Music Hall.

Like Britain, America developed Vaudeville out of various component parts, but they were different parts. Although 'singing while you eat' was as common in America as elsewhere, the population in the frontier towns was less settled, less married and less constrained by the expectations of family and responsibility. There was consequently a greater social function for the brothel – as opposed to the more independent street-walkers of London – and it was often the brothels (with their wine-check girls, their madames, and their facilities for heavy spending by the 'boys just in town after four months on the range') that became the location for the 'specialist shows'. Before the Civil War these audiences wanted sexier, cruder and more female material than the urbanized, family-based English working class. This led to the development of 'the only indigenous art-form of America', the Chorus Line, or Tights Show, in which girls were introduced more for what they looked like than for what they did. In 1866 the first real Tights Show, *The Black Crook*, ran for sixteen months in New York, and business boomed. Quickly plot was eliminated, and the pattern of American burlesque was established for the next half century: a format based on the minstrel shows, but with 'the girls' replacing the minstrels. They would perform a mixture of comedy patter interspersed with singing and dancing as an opening number. The same girls would appear in the last section of the show, the 'afterpiece', which was usually some sort of skit, and was intensely and directly sexual. In between there would be the *olio* (from a Spanish word meaning 'mixture'), a Variety Show with the emphasis on speciality acts rather than on the singing and dancing which were the backbone of British Music Hall. This format was made, of course, for exclusively male and distinctly unrefined audiences, who were by implication at least clients of the brothels.

For those with less money to spend and a desire for something less sexual, the Museums, a uniquely American form of entertainment, developed. The offered an odd combination of freak-show and Variety Performance, and were often substantial establishments. The customers first visited the 'curio hall' where, presented in scientific terms, they would be able to view oddities of nature ranging from pickled embryos to Siamese twins. More elaborate Museums also included waxworks of famous personalities. After the curios the customers would proceed to the show, which lasted thirty or forty minutes. The shows were usually performed from tiny stages: 'when we played a war piece, everybody had to be private: there wasn't room to get a general's epaulettes through the stage entrance'; and they were almost exclusively confined to solo acts. Museum work was punishingly hard (so much so, that there were never animal acts since the animals could not have taken the pace). If the curio show proved attractive, the performers were known to repeat their acts up to seventeen times a day because new customers could not be let in until the previous lot were moved on. The performers also worked under other sorts of restrictions: the Museums depended for their success on attracting mixed audiences and appearing 'respectable' and 'scientific' (though obviously there were con men of all sorts, as Mark Twain's *Huckleberry Finn* makes clear). So a great list of words were forbidden, including not just swearing ('damn', 'hell' and 'sucker') but various rather peculiar taboos such as 'bedbugs' and 'socks'.

There remained, however, a gap between the vulgarity of burlesque and the discomfort and physical crush of the Museum. And in 1881 this gap was filled as D. Gilbert points out, by one man's imaginative amalgamation of apparently disparate elements:

The Vaudeville we know was sired by Tony Pastor who first played to a 'double audience' [both sexes] when he opened his 14th St House in Tamany Hall, New York, on October 24th, 1881. It was the first 'clean' vaudeville show in America and to its bill, as Fred Stone used to say, a child could take its parents. To Pastor go the honors for tossing variety's denimed frowsiness into the trashcan and bringing out My Lady Vaudeville in starched organdy — a shiny child washed behind the ears.[22]

Tony Pastor was a remarkable man. He was born, probably, in 1837. His father was a musician for Barnum and he had begun performing before he was six. Until the Civil War (1861) he was an all-purpose travelling showboy — singing, dancing, clowning, playing trumpet and acting as circus ringmaster from the age of fourteen. Despite all this he was curiously innocent and untouched (his worst expletive was said to be 'Why Jiminetty!'). After the war and the failure of his first theatre, he spent the 1870s taking a series of touring companies on the road through the small towns of the East Coast. He came back from these tours having learned about a whole new audience that no one in the business was catering to: Pastors, on 14th Street, was his response. At first he had to advertise widely to attract a female clientele and even gave away free gifts of sewing patterns and ribbons to those who came; but his idea swiftly took off; the Vaudeville concept expanded nationwide in the next ten years. He himself stayed downtown on 14th Street, even when it became unfashionable and financially unviable. Pastors stayed open until its founder died in 1908. He viewed the extraordinary success of his imitators with apparent pleasure, while saying that he wouldn't care for the responsibility of the big circuits and huge houses developed by Keith, Weber and Field (once his own protegés) and Hammerstein.

He was also the first of the Americans to go to Europe in search of new talent. In 1894 he finally persuaded Vesta Tilley to come and work for him. He had been trying to pull this off since the mid-1880s, but for some reason her father had always strongly opposed the idea of her working in America. (Was this because he felt he did not know America well enough to maintain his control? Or fear of the vanquished American boyfriend? Or worry at leaving his family?) He was convinced that her work would not be well-received there, despite the fact that Pastor had opened his first show with a male-impersonator, Ella Wesner, who sang masher songs with considerable characterization. While it was true that a number of British stars 'flopped' in the States, Pastor's judgements were usually accurate. Now, however, Vesta Tilley was ready and willing: in 1894 Pastors was at the height of its fame; he offered her a six-week unbroken booking and a handsome fee; in addition he paid her travelling expenses in full, including the price of her dresser. She was not, of course, the first British artiste he had invited, but she was to be one of his most successful.

She arrived in the States to discover his considerable talent for publicity: he had arranged for the fullest press coverage of her arrival at the docks and had organized an immensely strong line-up of American talent to appear with her, while giving her top billing as 'England's Greatest Comedienne'.

Vesta Tilley was alarmed by this extravagant hype: she was afraid it might raise audience expectations too high and she was particularly nervous to discover that she was to follow Lottie Gilson, 'The Little Magnet', current darling of New York Vaudeville. She felt that it would be nearly impossible to follow so beloved a performer. (Lottie Gilson had introduced a stylistic innovation into her act — 'the stoodge singer', a member of the audience who entered into the song with her, putting in relevant lines and leading the chorus. This innovation suggests the more 'professional' nature of American Vaudeville; in England, where audience participation was a key part of Music Hall, most performers spent more time trying to shut up their volunteer assistants than they did planting them in the audience.)

The first song that Vesta Tilley sang in America was 'The Boys of the Racketty Club', describing a hectic evening among the upper-class swells of West End Clubland. She wore Hunt Ball evening dress: red dresscoat, knee breeches, white waistcoat and tie. It was a mistake, accommodating neither the different social make-up of her audience (which was aspirant — as opposed to a London audience, which was either sufficiently upper class as to afford a joke against itself, or sufficiently poor to enjoy the ridicule) nor to the foreignness of the images. From all accounts it was experience and determination that got her through the number. After the change, however, she did a seaside white flannels and boater number and was an instant success. After that the audience loved her: she sang six songs, was on stage for over an hour, made a speech and received a congratulatory welcome from the Elite Club of New York. She was embraced on stage by Tony Pastor and knew that she was going to make it.

In New York, far more than in London, Vaudeville came under the serious scrutiny of professional critics. Epes

Sargent, under the pen name of Chicot, had first started Vaudeville criticism in the mid-1880s with a column called 'Chatter from Music Halls'. (He never thought Vesta Tilley more than 'an ordinary entertainer'.) Thanks to his initiative, Vaudeville lived under the same critical tyranny as straight theatre did, and does. One of the most influential members of the New York fraternity in the 1890s was an Englishman, Alan Dale. He was notorious for his harsh judgements on English performers, and Vesta Tilley awaited his verdict anxiously. For once it was favourable and he dubbed her 'The Irving of the Halls': this rather grand title, which would have pulled no weight with London Music Hall audiences, became her sobriquet in America. It was taken up adoringly by other journalists. For example, in the *Concert Goer* in 1903 Channing Ellery wrote:

The Irving of the Halls is the name bestowed on Vesta Tilley by the well-known newspaper writer Mr Alan Dale in a moment of justifiable enthusiasm. For my own part I find Miss Tilley a far more entertaining and engaging person than Henry Irving. I find her art fully as true − truer indeed if I dare say it − and herself endowed with infinitely more personal magnetism than the famous actor can boast of in his make-up.[23]

(In the *Recollections* Vesta Tilley quotes this article in full, apparently just in order to pooh-pooh the idea.)

Her six-week tour was an enormous success. She quickly learned what New York audiences liked and gave it to them. They came to love her 'masher' songs − the dandy songs of high-styled young men, which she was already singing less of at home. She began to set fashions for the young dandies of America − for instance her 'Algy' costume was a pale grey morning coat and preposterously embroidered waistcoat which she had bought at auction on the death of Lord Anglesey. In London this outfit was meant to suggest the extreme affectation of her hero; in America it was perceived as the height of European chic, and taken up by fashion-conscious young men and a real vogue for grey morning coats developed. (The fashion was shipped back to Europe after the First World War.) Likewise, on one occasion she came off the stage for a quick change and discovered that her maid had forgotten the cuff-links. Vesta Tilley was obsessively precise about her costuming and would never wear fakes with back fastenings, nor would she perform without cuff-links. She snatched the ribbons from her maid's hair and tied them as cuff-links. A few weeks later she saw replicas of the ribbons in a smart men's wear shop, labelled as the latest cuff-links from London, 'as worn by Vesta Tilley'.

The idea of merchandizing appealed enormously to Vesta Tilley and Walter de Frece. In London, stars sold their photographs for postcards, of which there was an enormous turnover, but there were few other ways of creating spin-off industries. In America, the commercial and advertising potential seemed much greater, and she was, if not the inventor, then one of the first exploiters of this profitable business. That year in New York she licensed the Vesta Tilley Boater, with white satin band, to a women's millinery shop, and a Vesta Tilley Vest (waistcoat), Vesta Tilley Cigars and Vesta Tilley Socks for the male market. She also successfully sold her name for use in promoting sheet music; her own songs sold well, particularly her American number, 'The Man who Broke the Brokers', specially written by W. Jerome which she had commissioned after a visit to the New York Stock Exchange. This was an enormous hit, precisely because she was impersonating the ambitions of a great section of her audience.

After this first visit, Vesta Tilley returned six times to America. Apart from her professional reception, it is clear that both she and Walter enjoyed the greater class mobility and they formed many close and enduring friendships with Americans outside the theatrical profession in a way they did not seem able to do in England. Eventually Pastors proved too small to pay her enough, and, apparently with Tony Pastor's own help and support, she signed with Weber and Field. She had in fact accepted a contract from

Hammerstein's agent, at £1,000 a week, but when the great man himself visited London he decided on the strength of one late-night show that she was not worth the fabulous fee. Instead of arguing with him, Walter de Frece quickly accepted a Weber and Field offer for the same sum, though without telling Hammerstein. He then agreed to cancel the contract for a substantial consideration. She first appeared for Weber and Field at their Broadway house in 1903, with many of the greatest stars of American Vaudeville: Lilian Russel, Ross and Fenton and May Irwin — who with her songs 'Frog Song' and 'New Bully' introduced ragtime to the East Coast, and hence the world.

She and Walter also created their own show, 'The Vesta Tilley Vaudeville Company', and took it on the road through Buffalo, Philadelphia, Baltimore, Chicago, Cleveland, Boston, Detroit, Pittsburg, Cincinnati, Washington, Toronto in Canada and minor towns *en route*, touring for over a year. After disbanding the highly successful road show, she presented a range of performances: *Algy*, a specially written farce based on the 'Piccadilly Johnnie with the Little Glass Eye' which had proved so successful on tour; and a three-week engagement in Boston as a 'front stage act' (performing as in Pantomime, in front of the curtain, between the acts of a popular comedy *There and Back* by George Arliss). She also renewed the possibility of performing women's roles by starring in the title role of an operetta *My Lady Molly* at Daly's in New York. A number of Vaudeville performers, like Lilian Russel, went on to 'make it' as straight actors in Musical Comedy, a feat practically unheard of in England. Vesta Tilley must have been tempted to remain permanently in America, just as later many Music Hall performers like Charlie Chaplin (who co-billed with Vesta Tilley several times on the Halls in Britain) were to do. Walter de Frece's interests, however, were based more firmly in Britain; not only was he the owner of a growing chain of Halls, he was also beginning to pursue political ambitions.

The 1890s and 1900s were the years that represented the

peak of Vesta Tilley's professional career, and saw the fullest flowering of the Music Hall. However, all the factors that were to lead to the breakdown of Music Hall were already emerging. In 1896 Bioscope was introduced as a 'Music Hall turn', just one more 'speciality act', about as popular as conjurors or animal acts. The 1890s also saw the growth of revue and to match it Music Hall increased the number of 'sketches' − tiny, complete dramas performed among the other turns. Music Hall was getting rich, and greedy: theatres became grander, individual acts increasingly elaborate, settings more lavish and the troupes in turn became larger.

But no one seemed worried; indeed the management and the more successful stars were profiting from the upswing. Vesta Tilley was one of them. She was not isolated from the changes in Music Hall, and indeed sometimes gave up her solo status to perform in the new sketches: Fred Karno and his company employed her for a sketch called 'The Mumming Birds'; the young Stan Laurel and Charlie Chaplin both appeared in this sketch. Vesta Tilley also devised a highly melodramatic sketch of her own in which she acted out the suicide of the poet Chatterton. That such a highbrow theme could be played straight for Music Hall indicates some of the changes that had taken place since its earliest days.

Vesta Tilley and her husband left London each year immediately after the Pantomime run for the South of France and returned in the late spring. In France they moved more easily in higher class society than was possible at home, and as Walter de Frece began to get more deeply involved in Conservative Party politics the weight of his Music Hall connections was clearly a growing burden. With Alfred Butt, Edward Moss and Oswald Stoll he became increasingly committed to raising the tone of Music Hall, and he was involved with Stoll in the creation of the Coliseum which opened in 1904, where Stoll realized his final dream. Although technically a Music Hall, it was designed like a theatre, no alcohol could be consumed on the premises and Stoll covered the walls backstage with notices reading, 'Please do not use strong language here' and 'Coarseness and vulgarity are not allowed in the Coliseum'. So fanatical was he about the moral standard of his Hall that he would never let Marie Lloyd appear there. Even after the war he maintained his standards and in 1926 personally brought the curtain down on Sophie Tucker, 'The Last of the Red Hot Mammas'. Incensed, she screamed at him, 'Mr Stoll, you should not be the manager of a vaudeville theatre — you should be a Bishop.'[24] But he and his friends were more and more setting the tone of major city Music Hall and some of the stars, of whom Vesta Tilley was a notable leader, enjoyed the upgrading of their profession and their social standing.

Vesta Tilley's principal performance remained as it always had been, but her skill and her fame were increasing. She now had in George Dance, E. W. Rogers, Joseph Tarbar and Oswald Stoll himself, some of the best song-writers available, and she had the power to buy their works exclusively. (One of the few professional regrets she ever expressed was over her failure to buy Katy Lawrence's great hit, 'Daisy Bell' with its now famous chorus 'Daisy, Daisy, give me your answer do', which Harry Dacre wrote in 1892. Vesta Tilley considered this 'the best Music Hall chorus ever written' and one which would have suited her act perfectly.) She continued to introduce new material constantly, unlike many of the performers, who as the length of the 'turns' got shorter (to accommodate the new 'two separate performances an evening' fashion) became increasingly dependent on repeating their major hits. In 1894 she was honoured by a 'Private Command': she was invited to perform for the Prince and Princess of Wales at a private party they were attending. Edward VII was a keen appreciator of Music Hall and as Prince of Wales and later as King summoned individual performers to appear before him, occasionally at Sandringham and more frequently at his friends' homes; he also attended performances incognito until his accession, but throughout his reign obviously considered it impossible to be seen in any Music Hall.

Towards the end of the century, recording for the gramophone provided a new source of income for Music Hall artistes and Vesta Tilley made a substantial number of records (however, few of these early recordings have survived as they were cut in soft wax and were extremely frail). In the first decade of this century Music Hall stars were also a natural choice for leading parts in the silent movies. Vesta Tilley worked twice with cinema producers, once with Walter Gibbons (later knighted) in what was a primitive experiment in 'talkies'. Gibbons was trying to find a way of synchronizing gramophone records with silent film reel. Vesta Tilley spent a good deal of time working with him on this project (which was unsuccessful); she was obviously aware of the future of film.

She also made a full-length feature with G. B. Samuelson. The scenario was based on her own song, 'Jolly Good Luck to the Girl Who Loves a Soldier', and was filmed at the Isleworth Studios. The film was intended to play with the images of her male-impersonations, so she acted all the parts, both the hero soldier and the heroine, a daughter of a multi-millionaire, plus a role as a hospital nurse. In these days before stunt actors, she had to gallop on horseback, ride a motor bicycle and bayonet German troops in the trenches. She found she loathed the experience of filming, particularly the business of repeating scenes endlessly and the long hours of work. As a scrupulous perfectionist in her own act it is surprising that she did not more enjoy the control over production that film technology might have given her: perhaps she did not like working within a cooperative endeavour, and under a director as opposed to on her own. Perhaps it was simply too physically taxing. Certainly she rejected all future offers, despite the chance to play sustained characterization, and to make excellent movies.

The enormous profits being turned by the managements of Music Halls, and the growth of the syndicates (groups of theatres owned by single companies) was putting pressure on individual performers. While Vesta Tilley (probably the highest paid woman on the Halls) was now earning about £500 a week, Harry Lauder up to £1,000 and stars like Little Tich and Marie Lloyd in excess of £300, they were definitely the minority. Managements now proposed a change in the contracting system which would have cut seriously into performers' wage packets: single-fee bookings for all theatres under single management and 'exclusive' use of the stars. This would have meant an end to the business of performing in more than one theatre a night and would have pinned individuals down for long periods in the suburban houses, preventing them from making high salaries in West End venues. In 1906 the various unions concerned, The Variety Artistes Federation, the National Union of Stage Workers and the Amalgamated Musicians Union, formed an alliance and tried to black the Halls of the more bullish managers. For the strike to be effective it clearly required the participation of the great stars, as well as the lesser performers and the backstage staff. Vesta Tilley's position in this was complicated: she was, in personal terms, far more closely associated with the managers than with fellow performers – her husband and friends were all on the other side. She initially voted against the strike. However when, from 1 January 1907, the alliance called out its members she felt disinclined to separate herself entirely from the strike, particularly since her great rival Marie Lloyd was making an enormous success of her role as strike leader. Vesta Tilley was continually pressed for her views by the press. She steered a delicate, middle-of-the-road course: 'I have no complaints, but I know other artistes have.' In her *Recollections* she writes off the strike as a 'little silliness', but in fact the management was forced to yield to at least some of the strikers' demands.

By 1911 the power of 'respectable Variety' emerged victorious. Edward Moss decided that the time was right for a special Variety Performance to be held at the Empire in Edinburgh for the King and Queen. (Edinburgh was less sensitive than London, being altogether a more 'respectable' town.) Unfortunately, after the plans were laid, the Empire burned to the ground during a performance, killing nine members of the audience and 'The Great Lafayette, the Illusionist' whose act had caused the conflagration. Moss, although enormously distressed, immediately started searching for another venue, and finally cooperated with Walter de Frece and Oswald Stoll in a formal Royal Command Variety Performance at the Palace Theatre in London.

Although the Royal Command Performance of 1912 represented a real achievement for Music Hall, the occasion itself was not a complete success. Trouble started with the bill itself; or rather the omissions from it. By far the most shocking was the absence of Marie Lloyd. Later wisdom may say, 'The only surprise was that anyone really expected her to be on it . . . by official moral standards of the time she was clearly unacceptable'. This refers not just to the content of her act, but perhaps even more to her 'private life' — she had been divorced twice and was currently living with her lover. It would have been impossible to expect the King to meet her, or even watch her perform. But at the time her exclusion was seen by her many adoring fans as incomprehensible or even vicious. Even after the fuss about her omission, and that of Albert Chevalier, one of the greatest exponents of the coster — or cockney — comedy songs so popular on the Halls ('historically and artistically the omission of Albert Chevalier was a blunder of the first magnitude', wrote the *Morning Post*) and of Eugene Stratton, 'the dandy coloured Coon', the show itself was not very exciting. Oswald Stoll was totally obsessed with respectability, even publishing an 'Advertisement' in the *Era* on the morning of the show, warning that 'Coarseness and vulgarity are not allowed. The Licensing Authorities forbid this and the great majority of the public resent it. This intimation is only rendered necessary by a few artistes'. The rehearsals turned into a nightmare. One advertised turn, Ida and Crispi Farren walked out when they were told that it was not 'very nice' for Ida to be rolled in a carpet and carried offstage.

For Vesta Tilley, whose place on the bill was assured both

by popular demand and by her husband's managerial role, the show was a débâcle. When she appeared in her trousers Queen Mary turned to the other ladies of the Court and all of them buried their faces in their programmes, keeping themselves pure from the shocking sight of female legs. It may also have been unfortunate that she chose 'Algy' — an old song by now — and 'Mary and John', presumably as a compliment to Oswald Stoll who had written it. The former may have been less acceptable to the royal party, aping as it did follies of their class, than one of her many popular numbers which mocked the pretensions of the lower-middle class. 'Mary and John' had never been one of her greatest hits.

Meanwhile, down the road, Marie Lloyd was socking it to her audience while outside the Shaftesbury hoardings read 'Every Performance by Marie Lloyd is a Command Performance by Order of the British Public'.

The personal message for Vesta Tilley and Walter de Frece must have been clear: despite their best efforts to raise the tone of Music Hall and disassociate themselves from its more raffish aspects, they were still excluded from the social milieu in which they wanted to live. Without in any way reducing her performing schedule, the couple began to look for a social base outside the theatrical world. Walter, whose financial and administrative ability had been used extensively over the years within the Conservative Party, began to make more public appearances; he spoke extensively up and down the country, particularly on financial and Empire issues, and his experience in what working-class audiences might like stood him in good stead as a popular orator. So did his good humour and experience of being heckled: on one platform he announced 'I am an Empire Man, when I die the word Empire will be found carved on my heart', and a voice in the audience called out, 'What about Hippodrome?' — since his theatres had always been called that, while the Empire had been the name of the chain owned by his friend and rival, Edward Moss. In his more public self-presentation his wife's popular appeal was not overlooked. In 1913 she went back to Worcester for the first time in twenty-five years to open the Worcester Women's Conservative Party Fête, and at the same time she gave a charity performance. Increasingly she appeared with Walter on his platforms, gave charity performances and organized philanthropic — and well-advertised — events.

And increasingly she also sang and presented 'patriotic' material in her own stage performance. Music Hall had always supplied the public with patriotic songs and from about 1912, following the national mood, these became increasingly militant. After the outbreak of the war in 1914 many Music Hall stars chose to 'do their bit' by raising morale and singing patriotic songs. Vesta Tilley was in the forefront of this drive: she spoke from recruiting platforms and sang a large number of 'soldier songs'. These were particularly welcomed because the sailor had a far more positive image than the infantryman, and too many volunteers in the early days of the war preferred the 'senior service'. She had an enormous success in this capacity, as she did selling War Bonds, and boosting morale on the Home Front with a string of humorous military 'types' presented on stages throughout the country. She also used her name and talent in support of numerous war effort charities — in 1916, for example, she appeared in an 'all star' fund-raising performance of J. M. Barrie's *The Admirable Crichton*, with some of the greatest names from 'straight' theatre: Gerald du Maurier, Gladys Cooper, Fay Compton, Ellen Terry, Ellen Tree and Madge Titheridge were also part of the cast. For such a company to admit a Music Hall artiste into its ranks shows both the effects of the war, and the success of Vesta Tilley's social advancement. Barrie consented to write in a 'page-boy' part expressly for her in this production.

Vesta Tilley never travelled overseas to perform for soldiers in the field; with unusual self-consciousness she went out of her way in her *Recollections* to explain the great difficulties of transporting all her necessary equipment. However, she did make a particular contribution to the well-being of wounded troops, touring military hospitals tirelessly and involving herself in charity shows to raise money for hospital funds and rehabilitation schemes.

She was by no means alone in this militaristic enthusiasm, and even stars with far more radical tendencies turned into good patriots from 1914.

While she spoke from recruiting platforms and sang the famous chorus beginning 'Girls if you want to love a soldier, you can all love me', Walter de Frece, invalided out of the Sportsman's Battalion, was appointed 'Honorary Organizer of the King's Funds for the rehabilitation of discharged soldiers and sailors into civilian life'. He also organized entertainments for the forces and the munition workers.

This proved infinitely more successful as a form of social advancement than organizing Royal Command Performances. In 1919 he was knighted in the New Year's Honours List, and in the same year Vesta Tilley announced her 'final tour' before retirement. Walter de Frece wanted to go into Parliament and knew that this would be impossible with a wife 'on the Halls'. In addition, Vesta Tilley was now fifty-six years old, and although still an immense draw at any theatre she chose to grace, she must have known it could not last forever. Moreover the war had changed radically the representation of women; the Queen, who had covered her eyes at Vesta Tilley's performance in 1912, had since chatted to land army girls in breeches; the young men whom she had lovingly chided were dead, and the young women were wearing clothes that made them look boyish without dressing up. The first, ominous conversions of Music Halls into cinemas were beginning.

In April 1919 she announced to the press:

I really have engagements for the next six years, but my husband thinks I have worked long enough. I love my work so it will be hard to have to give it up when my position is greater than it has ever been, but my husband thinks it better to retire at the height of my success and to leave nothing I hope but pleasant memories behind with my public, and I think he is right . . . The only time I will come out of my retirement will be to sing for some charitable cause.[25]

Throughout the final tour (interrupted only by her husband's by-election for the seat of Ashbury-under-Lyme for which she broke off performing and went to assist him to victory, proving herself an unusually effective canvasser), she laid heavy emphasis on well-publicized charitable activities. She presented £500 in War Bonds to the mayors of all the principal cities she visited — Liverpool, Edinburgh, Manchester, Nottingham, Bradford, Sheffield and Birmingham amongst them. She endowed cots in children's hospitals in Blackpool and Manchester and attracted audiences throughout the country.

She completed her farewell tour, very properly, with four weeks at Oswald Stoll's Coliseum. She played her final night there in June 1920. It was a moving tribute to a great artist and the reporting of it must have seemed a final benediction:

There are many reasons for the pre-eminence Miss Vesta Tilley enjoys. She has, through a long stage career, always given of her best and bountifully . . . She has stood with the clean wholesome song through periods when a great number of her rivals have gained applause and kudos by the suggestive and vulgar . . . She has come through with a record for healthy and generous fun-giving unfurnished by any concession to the vulgar or prurient. It was the public appreciation of her high ideals and delightful art which were poured out in the exuberant welcome and lingering farewell which the grand audience gave her tonight.

The demonstration that followed [her performance] was without precedent in music hall history. It mingled with warm admiration of an artistic genius, warm appreciation of a personality such as the royal donations announced yesterday for the alleviation of suffering of the halt and maimed.[26]

Her last song, 'Jolly Good Luck to the Girl who Loves a Soldier', received a forty-minute ovation, and Ellen Terry, the most popular serious actress of the time, came on stage to embrace Vesta Tilley and make a short speech. Nearly two million individuals had signed 'The People's Tribute', which was presented in bound volumes and opened with an ecstatic eulogy:

Your songs have stirred great multitudes . . . you have been a picture of home to lonely soldiers . . . It may be said of your retirement that it will eclipse the gaiety of nations.[27]

Vesta Tilley left the stage weeping. It was over. That night she disappeared absolutely and forever. From the dressing-room Lady de Frece emerged, the gracious wife of the Conservative MP who cut his connections with Music Hall so rigorously that he was nicknamed 'Sir Altered de Frece' by his critics.

Her husband was Member of Parliament first for Ashbury and later for Blackpool. Lady de Frece was presented at the last Drawing-Room of the 1923 season; they were much to be seen in high society, at the races and the opera, at state balls and garden parties. He was appointed a Deputy Lieutenant of Lancashire in 1924 and they entertained lavishly. In 1932 he retired because of ill health and they went to live in Monte Carlo. He died there on 8 January 1935, leaving her a widow after forty-five years of marriage. Although she lived on, a respected philanthropic lady, until 16 September 1952, her health was delicate and her spirits never recovered. By the time she died she was eighty-eight and her memory had faded; even the medium she used had vanished; the era she had represented and in some ways symbolized was gone.

Every year on her birthday the Covent Garden flower-sellers sent her a bunch of violets. She had never consciously represented their interests; she had never sought their friendship. But, almost without her will or consent, she represented something important for an enormous number of people, especially women, throughout her working life. She had played with the boundaries of gender definition at a time when those boundaries were wobbling and the definitions themselves were up for grabs. Beyond her own, rather limited, personality she was a crucial cultural sign of her times. What was that magic?

FRONT CLOTH

The very nature of Vesta Tilley's life and work raises important questions for us now. She focuses attention on issues of sexuality and gender representation. She was also, visibly, a very successful woman. More than that: she was a star, one of the first international stars of popular culture. She was a star where she should not have been one. Tampering, whether consciously or unconsciously, with the very deeply held Victorian myth that the division between the genders was natural, immutable and absolute, she still managed to overcome the severe personal disadvantages with which she was born — in terms of class, sex, financial and educational background. Even her physical appearance, so unfashionably slight, should have militated against her success. She achieved exactly what she set out to achieve. She was not just an extremely successful, and rich, professional woman (in the second half of the 1890s she was probably the most highly paid working woman in Britain), she also managed to attract both public respect and personal happiness. Even a century later this is no mean achievement, yet she managed it with very little going for her except a reasonable ear for music, a sharp eye for detail and an iron will. Unlike many women of her own time — as of ours — she was not afraid of her own success, nor was she obsessed by it. She refused even to acknowledge that the old conflict between career and personal life existed; nor did she let herself become a victim of her own emotional desires: they were always well and effectively channelled. She made in her own, not unreasonable, terms a very wise and satisfactory marriage, one which not only 'allowed' her to pursue her professional life, but which actually enhanced it, and also enhanced her social ambitions and appears to have made her very happy; within the constraints of her own social milieu it was obviously an extraordinarily successful partnership.

It is important not to under-estimate what she pulled off against such apparently impossible odds. Obviously all Music Hall artistes were economically exploited by the Hall owners and managements, but Vesta Tilley also took very direct control over the product of her labour and over the money that she made. She took direct action to own her act: she did not sing songs at the direction of any management, and even in her first appearance in Pantomime she insisted on changing the traditions of her role in order to present herself as she thought fit. She was attentive to questions of copyright and publication, and she was careful about her publicity material. She did not allow agents and middle-men to get rich off her talent and hard work; her father had, of course, lived off her labour, but after his death no one else ever had that sort of power again. In this sense, of course, her marriage was also wise: her husband was her agent and manager; but he always maintained his own commercial interests and was not dependent on her in any way.

I am also fascinated by her apparent ability to turn potential psychological difficulties to her own advantage. Given the lack of self-consciousness her *Recollections* display, and the distance in time and social conditions all my comments in this area have to be 'speculative', but certain aspects of her life cannot be ignored.

In *Joan of Arc*, Marina Warner raises an interesting idea: examining the history, both material and literary, of women's transvestism, she suggests that a possible trigger might be

Identification with the Father and the prohibition against incest . . . It would be interesting for a psychologist to pursue the reason that so many of the known historical cases are also illegitimate children. . . . The exchange of femininity for masculinity also marks a psychic identification with the lost father; in the case of Joan, when the rejection was voluntary, even longed for, it still had the effect of pushing her into imitative maleness, as if to defend herself against the strong emotions that clearly flowed between them. *La Fille d'un Roi* [a fourteenth-century mystery play] is a fascinating example of these unconscious impulses, for it reveals that the desire of a father for his daughter, or of a daughter for her father, can impel her to refuse her womanhood, to refuse to become an adult object of his lust and to retreat instead into a symbolic neutral state, neither fully man nor fully woman. By denying sexual differentiation the grown-up state is never reached.[1]

In terms of Vesta Tilley's biography this causality does seem suggestive: Vesta Tilley, quite unnecessarily − since she was doing very well singing female roles − felt a strong urge to cross-dress just at the time when she was being asked to act as an adult − specifically to undertake the financial support of her family. At the same time she was being removed from a family environment into one of extraordinary intimacy with her father, who had apparently chosen her as his favourite child, and even as a love object preferred to her mother. The total obliteration of her mother from her *Recollections*, and indeed apparently from her life, does suggest that this was not the easiest transition. If the wearing of male clothes was a protection against her feelings for her father, or indeed his for her, then it has to be seen as a brilliant solution. It gave her all the advantages of her position − exclusive rights to her father's company, escape from her mother, a professional life which gave her prestige both in his eyes and in the eyes of the world − whilst signing her rejection of a heterosexual interest between them.

In the same way her careful construction of a public persona so radically different from her stage persona gained her 'the best of all worlds': she could express 'masculinity' and enjoy its power, without having to reject her own 'femininity' or endure the social stigma attached to women who are too 'mannish'. She could also enjoy, and obviously did, a certain amount of lesbian-orientated devotion from her fans without having to take any responsibility for it. Her *Recollections* are illuminating on the rare occasions when she acknowledges this sort of devotion. She patently did enjoy the power that she had, but managed at the same time to be dismissive (if not insulting) about its motivation. She tells two stories in particular. One concerns a woman who presented her with a ten-year diary in which she had recorded her every encounter with Vesta Tilley, Vesta Tilley's work and Vesta Tilley memorabilia. Vesta Tilley claims to have found this faintly amusing, but reading between the lines, it becomes clear that she accepted the woman's gift of the diaries and kept them at least until 1934 when she wrote the *Recollections*. Another story is about a woman who came to watch her perform nightly for a three-week run and sent endless messages backstage asking for an interview. Vesta Tilley, who is the only source of this tale, claims that she finally invited the woman to her dressing-room, but was careful to receive her with her hair in the little rat's-tail plaits that she used under her wig and her face smeared in cold-cream, clad in a dressing-gown. When the woman went into ecstasies and proclaimed that she knew Vesta Tilley had made herself such a fright in 'order to test her devotion' the star was able to shrug her off as a lunatic. But she tells both anecdotes in considerable detail — carefully separated by the devotion of another, heavily pregnant woman who wanted to see her perform and delivered twins within hours of the performance for which Vesta Tilley had provided her with free tickets. (She called one child Vesta, the other Tilley, and Vesta Tilley stood as godmother to them both.) Clearly it was important to her that her readers should know how deeply devoted to her other women were, and — at the same time — should also know that she found such devotion risible. From a contemporary point of view this is not an attractive characteristic. There is no evidence whatsoever that Vesta Tilley was a lesbian, or that she particularly craved emotional intimacy with other women − she did not, for example, have close women friends, despite the fact that 'passionate friendships' were quite acceptable for women of her time. However, from a totally individual perspective this was a shrewd psychological ruse: in her 'stage persona' she could attract an almost slavish devotion from other women, which her 'private' or 'true' persona was at liberty to dismiss, or even mock.

As I have already suggested, she even turned the occasion of her illness to a similar, personal advantage. For the rest of her life she was regarded as frail, in need of rest and special care. Given the fact that she fulfilled a gruelling professional schedule of travel and performance for thirty years after her serious illness of 1890 − and lived till the age of 88, it is difficult to believe that she was really in such delicate health, but the advantages that effectively accrued to her through her illness cannot be denied.

In this context it is perhaps important to look at the fact that Vesta Tilley and Walter de Frece did not have children. Given her profound personal reticence in the *Recollections*, supported by the discretion of the press, it is impossible to know why they did not have children. I cannot escape the feeling that Vesta Tilley's illness, given its duration, the special tenderness with which both Walter de Frece and public opinion treated her subsequently and the few clues available from the information about her treatment, was gynaecological. It is possible that, within months of getting married, she produced symptoms that made it impossible − or dangerous − for her to have children. It is also possible that she and Walter de Frece made a decision about this and were, like many others in her society, consistent and efficient users of contraception: that information was certainly available to financially successful middle-class couples by 1889. It is hard to guess how, or even whether, Vesta Tilley would have been able to maintain her 'double life' if she had had children. Without them she was able to present herself both as perfect wife ('private persona') and as perfect androgyne ('stage persona'). Given the constraints on 'perfect femininity' of late nineteenth-century society, it would have been hard for her to have found a way of presenting herself as *perfect mother* in addition to all her other immaculate roles. Vesta Tilley was always careful to be seen as 'motherly', as properly maternal: her involvement in children's charities in the post-war years has already been mentioned. She did more than endow cots in hospitals; from 1900 onwards she was conspicuous not just for her donations of cash, but for the charitable benefits she gave and for the charitable children's parties she both subsidized and personally attended at her own homes. In 1903, while she was in America, she became involved in an incident which had international ramifications: she adopted the cause of an Inuit boy named Mene Wallace, who, with his family, had been brought to New York from the Polar regions of Canada by Commander Peary (an internationally renowned explorer). American urban life had destroyed the family group. After his relatives had died, and he had discovered that his father's bones were on public display in the Natural History Museum, the boy had run away. Vesta Tilley, on hearing this strange tale, had personally employed a detective agency to find the youth, and when this was successful, had him brought to New York and cared for. The subsequent publicity was embarrassing to the American government – though completely favourable towards Vesta Tilley. The youth was finally returned to his tribal homelands, whence he wrote ecstatic letters of gratitude to her and called her his 'white' mother. Although, cynically, the incident enhanced her reputation she also became involved financially at a time when this cannot have seemed a good investment. In the same way her championship of the *wounded* soldier after 1914 enhanced her image as 'maternal' and therefore 'naturally womanly'. This was both a sound choice as a publicity device, but also an investment of caring against a popular movement – which had tended to see the wounded as the write-offs of the war. If she knew that she was infertile, this devotion fits comfortably into a well-recognized pattern of substitution; if she was choosing to be child-free it also represents a perfectly normal way of allaying any guilt. None the less, it is impossible with any understanding of the climate in which she lived, not to recognize that there was a real 'use function' in the combination of freedom from both career and individuality-destroying responsibility, especially considering the social and professional role that she had chosen, which childlessness gave her.

It is important to remember that if Walter de Frece had not been satisfied with her as his wife, her childlessness, coupled with her professional activities, would have made it socially acceptable for him to terminate the marriage in circumstances which, however damaging to her, would not have affected his interests. Whatever their reasons they must have been known and shared by the couple.

I do not know, and do not believe that it is possible to know, why Vesta Tilley and Walter de Frece did not have children. All I want to stress here is Vesta Tilley's remarkable capacity for getting the best possible deal out of what was available to her. What is interesting is that none of her contemporary witnesses either criticizes or pities her for her childlessness: this suggests as much as anything her ability to play all aspects of her life with considerable skill to her own advantage.

Contemporary feminists are suspicious of individually successful women. In political terms that suspicion is justified but only if it acknowledges the extraordinary balance and skill required to combine in one life the multiple levels of success which Vesta Tilley managed to show herself capable of. Summarizing her career, I would have to say that although she is not a woman whom I find personally endearing, nor one whose choices I admire, I do have to acknowledge with admiration her skill at outmanoeuvring the societal disapproval and the inclination to unhappiness which threatened to dog every inch of her journey.

THE ACTRESS
IN LATE VICTORIAN
SOCIETY

Would any one of us wish our daughters to go on the stage?
There can be but one answer to this. 'No'!
  F. C. Burnand[1]

Acting provided 'the prospect of living the only free life a woman
can lead — the artistic one'.
  Eleanor Marx[2]

There has been very little attention paid, either by their
contemporaries or by subsequent historians, to the women
who supplied the voracious demands of Music Hall audiences
for new acts, songs and performers. There is an enormous
amount of anecdotal material, but very little sociological or
analytical study. Peter Davison's *The Songs of the British
Music Hall* is a notable exception to this, and his attempt to
analyse some of the better-known hits of the great Music Hall
era is extremely useful. But the gap remains, and seems a sad
one, for Music Hall was an enormously important and
influential part of working-class culture in the fifty years
before the First World War. A large number of women were
employed by the Halls, and with the expansion of the printed
mass media the Music Hall artistes represented ideals of
working-class 'femininity' in various forms; the public personae of the great stars — both onstage and increasingly in
their so-called 'private' lives — were a source of aspiration and
admiration. The scant available evidence suggests, more by
emphasizing the few exceptions than by affirming the norm,

that almost all the performers of the Halls were from working- or lower-class backgrounds. The Halls provided one of the very few ways in which such women could make a mark on a society which disenfranchised, impoverished and severely limited them in other ways.

This neglect is partly because the whole theatrical profession was regarded with considerable suspicion in the nineteenth century: although the 1911 census, for instance, lists 9,171 actresses in business, *The Handbook of Women's Work* of 1876 (a product of the mid-century feminist movement) makes no mention at all of this particular opening for paid work. The *Englishwoman's Journal* is nearly as silent, never according actresses the obituaries that other women in the public eye received and usually mentioning acting as a profession only in a cautionary way. Edwardians of all classes were voracious theatre-goers, but the increasingly serious attention paid to straight actresses by the end of the nineteenth century was actually at the further expense of Music Hall artistes: the theatre became more respectable and artistically serious in the 1860s and 1870s partly because the 'vulgar' audience was syphoned off — or took itself off — to the Halls, leaving the middle and upper classes to patronize the serious theatre again without fear of contamination. While the working-class women of talent were employed in the Halls, the more middle-class entrants to the acting professions were concerned with the more high-minded artistic productions, ranging from Shakespearean tragedy through drawing-room dramas to the new social question plays of Ibsen and subsequently Jones, Pinero, Shaw, Wilde and Barrie by the end of the pre-war period. Here, with an emphasis less on making a job of work, and more on personal self-expression, women were able to overcome some of the prejudices against the theatrical profession, but only by rigidly disassociating themselves from the Music Hall. In between the serious artistic theatre and the Music Halls were the Gaiety Girls of the Musical Comedies, patronized by the aristocracy. Here beauty and finding an appropriate patron were as important as talent. Between 1884 and 1914 there were nineteen marriages between actresses and members of the British aristocracy, including fourteen with peers of the realm. These women sang and danced, and represented highly sexual glamour on which the popular press fed. There is clearly a need for some scholarly sorting out here, as to how the groups were separated and allied, but the boundaries were clear; although a few women moved upwards from Music Hall to Musical Comedy — Ellaline Terris is one conspicuous example — there was very little crossing over; by and large the women in Music Hall were used by those further up the social scale as a foil for their own longed-for respectability. Even though the reputation of women on the stage did improve radically from the 1860s onwards, their respectability was always tenuous and had to be guarded rigorously.

The position of women was also affected by the social standing of theatre itself, which had a complex and shuffling journey towards artistic and social acceptability. Although Victorian puritanism tended to believe that acting was in and of itself a form of immorality and that the theatres were redolent with sexual corruption (prostitutes, to the annoyance of professional actresses, were always euphemistically described as 'actresses' in the press), this attitude varied considerably during the course of the nineteenth century. The middle classes had finally deserted the theatre at the very beginning of the nineteenth century, preferring either to patronize the opera or, better still, to stay at home with a novel or amateur musical performance. They felt they had been driven out by mob rule, which culminated in 1809 with the 'Old Price' Riots at the Drury Lane Theatre, after Kemble had converted one of the tiers into boxes to protect the gentry already driven out of the pit by the working classes and had also raised the price of tickets in the pit.

So effective and varied were the means of protest adopted by the rioters that for sixty-seven nights not a word of the entertainment offered by the company could be heard in the theatre. Ultimately

Kemble had to concede the substance of their demands, and make an abject apology for good measure. Small wonder that for the next fifty years polite society quitted the theatre.[3]

But despite its reputation for immorality and vulgarity, the young Queen Victoria and her Consort frequently attended the theatre in the 1840s and even appointed one of her favourite actresses, Caroline Heath — later Mrs Wilson Barret — as Reader to the Queen. Another actress admired by the Queen, Helena Faucit, married the Prince Consort's extremely respectable biographer, Sir Theodore Martin, and was a frequent visitor to the palace. Helena Faucit took a high moral tone about the theatre and considered drama to be a powerful moral influence. She worked, she said, 'to put in living form before an audience the types of noble womanhood as they have been revealed by our best dramatic poets, and especially by Shakespeare.'[4] Many of those who saw her act agreed with her about her moral worth and the value of her contribution. One critic admired particularly, 'the contagious elevation of thought and purity of sentiment proceeding from this young lady which, next to devotion itself, tends powerfully to confirm man in the paths of virtue.'[5]

Despite this encouraging start to Victoria's reign, the standing of actresses declined sharply over the next three or four decades. The confusion over the theatrical patents which led to the development of Music Hall also led to the debasement of serious theatre in the 1840s and 1850s. To escape from the monopoly of the patent theatres all other playhouses had to introduce music and circus to escape prosecution; the elements of spectacle attracted a less intellectual audience on which the theatres in turn became financially dependent, and thus ever less attractive to respectable audiences. In addition, the literary figures of the Romantic revival turned away from drama towards lyricism, perhaps because the playwright was regarded as subservient both to the principal performers and to the needs of theatrical presentation, and this was unacceptable to the new individualism and self-expression of the romantic view of the artist.

But there were other reasons why women acting came to typify vice in the minds of many Victorians. Although the other arts became increasingly respectable as pursuits for women, because they were not tainted with commercialism and because the romantic ideal of the artist as one purified by suffering and close to the truths of nature was quite compatible with nineteenth-century ideologies of femininity, acting had an intrinsic problem: by definition it had to be 'public' performance, and by the second half of the century 'decent' women were supposed neither to have nor to desire a public life, an audience beyond the home. The actress who not only displayed herself in public, but did so for money, was the very antithesis of the Victorian 'lady'.

Furthermore, women were believed to be the source and upholders of truth in society, and equally fundamentally they were at one with nature. Pretending to be someone else, the essence of acting, was both untruthful and unnatural; it involved artifice and deception, and therefore any woman who wanted to act was obviously deficient in womanliness.

The final moral danger in acting was that apart from some of the London theatres, such as the Savoy where women were taken on longer contracts, almost all professionals toured extensively, both in companies and as individuals. This was structurally inevitable in Music Hall, but it also tended to be true of other forms of theatrical engagement. In 1884 Mrs Kendal, an actress so respectable that she made it a public boast that she had never played opposite any man onstage other than her own husband, gave an address to the National Association for the Promotion of Social Science in which she preached the moral and social probity of the stage and its suitability as a profession for young women. She included the following rhetorical question:

How many educated girls finding themselves through force of circumstances suddenly compelled to face the world on their own account, have turned with relief from the stereotyped position of a 'companion' or a 'governess' to the vista that an honourable connection with the stage holds out to them?[6]

She had located precisely the fear that Victorian men had: that women would indeed be lured away from suitable domestic occupations into a mobile independence which was unacceptable. Her speech brought an immediate and virulent attack on the morals of the stage from numerous sources, all of whom felt that a well-brought-up girl would either find the morality of such a life repugnant or, worse, she would succumb to its corruption.

Until the 1860s almost all actresses in England came from theatrical families brought up on the stage and regarding it with a professionalism and straightforward familiarity. The majority of these families existed outside the normal social strata, laws unto themselves, and they usually married within their own caste. As late as the 1870s, Lady St Helier — an ambitious hostess and one of the first to introduce actresses and actors into 'Society' wrote that

the stage was a part of the community which lived on its own little world, entirely absorbed in its own professional interests and having no communication with any society outside its boundaries.[7]

Inevitably, these family groupings were tightly-knit since they saw themselves at odds with a respectable society which regarded them technically as 'rogues and vagabonds'. The remnants of this tradition can be found in the number of Music Hall stars who started out as part of a family act.

But the emergence of Music Hall broke this tradition, and by the 1870s most solo acts in Music Hall did not come from this old style theatrical family, although troupes often continued to. At the other end of the social spectrum, too, there had been an influx of more middle-class, non-theatrical family men into the profession in the late 1850s and 1860s, men like Henry Irving, Squire Bancroft, Charles Wyndham and John Hare (all of whom ended up with knighthoods, demonstrating the progress of the stage's upward mobility through the rest of the century). As they 'raised the tone' of the theatre and the lower classes deserted it for the Music Halls, there was a new space for women of a different social class to enter the profession. The needs of audience and actresses alike produced a shrewd response: the person perhaps most influential in creating a 'middle-class' theatre for the Victorian era was an actress, Marie Wilton — who later married Squire Bancroft, a famous actor-manager. Marie Wilton did come from a theatrical family, though a rather unusual one, as her father had run away from a respectable country family. She had grown up in the theatre and had made a considerable success in burlesque, notably in a male-impersonation role, Pippo, in a play written especially for her by H. J. Byron, *The Maid and the Magpie*, in 1859. Of her performance Dickens wrote to a friend:

I really wish you would go, between this and next Thursday, to see the *Maid and the Magpie* burlesque. There is the strangest thing in it that ever I have seen on stage. The boy, Pippo, by Miss Wilton. While it is astonishingly impudent (must be, or it couldn't be done at all) it is so stupendously like a boy, and unlike a woman, that it is perfectly free from offence . . . She does an imitation of the dancing of the Christy Minstrels — wonderfully clever — which in the audacity of its thorough-going is surprising. A thing that you *can not* imagine a woman doing at all; and yet the manner, the appearance, the levity, impulse and spirits of it are so exactly like a boy, that you cannot think of anything like her sex in association with it.[8]

In 1865 she managed to borrow £1,000 from a relative and go into theatre management. She obtained a run-down, unfashionably located theatre, the Queen's — nicknamed 'the Dustbowl' — but it was exactly what she required, mainly because it was small. She renamed it the Prince of Wales and here she created a radical departure from the usual theatres: an intimate, deliberately respectable theatre. Her innovations included chintz curtains for the boxes, a carpet on the floor of the stalls, white lace antimacassars on the backs of each seat, and a 'drawing-room' decor in tasteful pinks and blues. She launched a new sort of play for her new sort of audience: the 'cup and saucer' dramas of T. W. Robertson, delicate drawing-room comedies of manners. Robertson's plays made a total break, at least in style, with both the melodramas and the burlesques commonly available. Encouraged by Wilton, Robertson also developed the art of direction and stage management, submitting the actors both to the text and to the overall balance of the piece, and insisting on realistic scenery, complete in every detail. In particular, he looked to the staging of individual scenes to supply the nuances of meaning and emotion which words alone could not carry. This attention to precise detail led him to be described as 'a Pre-Raphaelite of the theatre'.

In the presentation of character his influence was immeasurable. He struggled to create both a more natural mode of acting and a more subtle degree of characterization to replace the heavy exaggeration of the mid-Victorian style and the 'stock characters' common to his time. His stage directions are heavy with warnings against the wild, melodramatic acting all-too-commonly regarded as necessary. In his play *MP* he directs the scene in which a bankrupt nobleman sees the sale of his mother's portrait:

The actor playing Dunscombe is requested not to make too much of this situation. All that is required is a momentary memory of childhood — succeeded by the external phlegm of a man of the world. No tragedy, no tears, no pocket handkerchief.[9]

This was a major change, and one which gradually percolated through the world of serious theatre. The Bancrofts having learned Robertson's lessons well, acted in his new style when they moved from the Prince of Wales to the far more important Haymarket. John Hare was clear about the debt to Robertson:

As nature was the basis of his own work, so he sought to make actors understand it should be theirs. He thus founded a school of natural acting which completely revolutionised the then existing methods, and by doing so did incalculable good to the stage.[10]

There are two reasons for giving considerable detail about the Robertson acting revolution. As his methods spread through the theatre they had a more general effect on audience expectation even at the level of Music Hall. It was clearly this taste for an unstrained, more natural performance that allowed Vesta Tilley's refined style of male-impersonation to take over in the 1890s from the more exaggerated and heavy swell impersonators like Millie Hylton, who had dominated the craft in the 1880s. The 'low key' delicate, and socially sophisticated satirical approach that Vesta Tilley perfected required an audience willing to see detail of characterization rather than just wanting the exaggerated, violent mockery of the burlesque.

Robertson's new type of play and presentation also had class implications. His work and that of his imitators required actresses who understood the social nuances of the society drawing-room in considerable detail: working-class actresses found it well nigh impossible to play these parts; roles that working-class women, or the old style professional actresses could not play were infinitely safer for middle-class women to attempt, because they would not risk losing caste by doing so. This did encourage the entry of middle-class women into the acting profession and by their entry they further emphasized the refinement of the new theatre.

Marie Wilton introduced other innovations too. Among them was the single-play bill. This permitted a later start, fitting in with middle- and upper-class dining hours, and an earlier finish, which gradually permitted actresses to take a fuller part in 'social life' than they had previously been able to do. Although the terms of their entry into society were not always straightforward, as T. H. S. Escott points out — 'Actresses are taken into society not professionally but on an unreal footing of equality which makes them more diverting'; and he criticized the 'prurient prudishness' with which hostesses treated these women[11] − none the less this new status made it still more possible for middle-class women to enter the profession without being cut off forever from their own roots. By the 1880s the monopoly of the old professional families had been broken: of the 145 actresses listed in Pascoe's *The Dramatic List* who had entered the profession in the 1860s and 1870s, only forty-five are identified as coming from theatrical families. By the end of the nineteenth century, professional actresses were complaining that the wings of the theatres 'stank of debs and Debrett'.[12]

The generation of respectability-conscious professionals like Marie Wilton, Mrs Kendal and Genevieve Ward was gradually replaced in serious drama by a new group of women, essentially middle class and highly conscious of their intellectual and artistic claims to self-expression. Many of them were anxious to find plays that afforded a genuine outlet to their political and social aspirations. It was women − in theatre management, as actresses and as audiences − who dominated the Ibsenite revolution of the 1890s and who took up Shaw's dramatic intentions with so much enthusiasm. These women, like Janet Achurch, Elizabeth Robins, Florence Farr and, of course, Mrs Patrick Campbell, may have had very different motives from the older 'respectables', but they were equally determined to separate themselves from the less respectable and 'trivial' actresses of the Halls and the Musical Comedies. They saw themselves primarily as artists and were seriously concerned with questions about the representation of women in culture.

Interestingly, many of them were overtly feminist and actively sought out, wrote and produced plays which presented the New Woman and the concerns of women like themselves. In 1908 they formed The Actresses Franchise League, specifically to bring their professional skills into the service of the suffrage cause. Cecily Hamilton, Sybil Thorndyke, Irene and Violet Vanburgh, along with Elizabeth Robins and others, were extremely active in the League. They were less afraid of and more practised at public speaking than many suffragists, and they wrote, marched and demonstrated for the vote. But their major contribution was the series of feminist, pro-vote plays, pageants and 'shows' that they wrote and produced throughout the country. These proved doubly successful both as propaganda and as fund-raisers. Previously the novel had been the major form by which many Victorian women had learned about ideas and ethics; now dramatic presentations were more accessible to them than pure theory and the effect of these dramas was acknowledged to be considerable. So although their ideals had changed, serious actresses were still highly conscious of the need to present that 'contagious elevation of thought and purity of sentiment' that Helena Faucit had demonstrated. They had, at some level, to justify the whole dubious business of having a public life by stressing their righteous service, moral standing and artistic importance. They were as cut off from the Gaiety Girls and the Music Hall artistes as the previous generation had been.

A conspicuous exception to this high-minded search for respectability was Ellen Terry 1847–1928. Although she was one of the most popular and brilliant of the serious actresses of her generation, playing in Shakespeare with Henry Irving and having a standing in both the profession and in society which was unique, she never took upon herself the mantle of public decency which her colleagues seemed to feel was necessary. She lived a boldly bohemian life-style: she had three brief marriages each lasting less than five years, and all ending in that ultimate Victorian disgrace, divorce. She had two illegitimate children and a series of close serious relationships with men, about which she showed no shame. Her beauty and her talent, and the growing desire of Victorian society to be titillated by a 'soupçon of naughtiness' plus her own personal warmth and magnetism gained her an extraordinary place in society, best summed up by Lady Salisbury's comment that her behaviour was 'never immoral only rather illegal'.

For many intelligent young women, including someone like

Eleanor Marx, she represented the possibility of a freer life-style which combined serious artistic purpose with personal liberation. She also overrode many of the social barriers imposed on actresses: she encouraged middle-class women to enter the profession; treated the stars of the Musical Comedies with the same respect that she proffered to her 'serious' colleagues; and displayed immense personal kindness and warmth towards the young and struggling — she adopted Ellaline Terriss, a Musical Comedy star who had come into the profession through the Music Halls, as her godchild after the death of Terriss's parents, sponsored her socially and gave her hard-headed advice, even when this earned her the dislike of managements. The fact that Ellen Terry was made a Dame in 1925 says as much about her individual achievements as it does about the social changes that the war brought about. But her standing also demonstrates clearly the class division between Music Hall and serious theatre at the beginning of the twentieth century. Marie Lloyd had an infinitely larger public following, was equally well-known for her warmth and goodness of heart, and had a private life no more scandalous than Terry's; but it was considered impossible to invite her even to perform at the Royal Command Variety Performance of 1912, and she died in relative poverty in the twenties, while Terry was honoured by the Crown.

It is important to stress the unique status that Ellen Terry enjoyed. When she appeared on stage at the Coliseum for Vesta Tilley's farewell performance in 1920 it was heralded by the press as an extraordinary event, emphasizing Vesta Tilley's pre-eminence and 'special' professional standing. But in retrospect, it also shows clearly the way that both women had been tokenized by the society that had privileged them: it was precisely because they were different from everyone else that they were allowed to break the rules. Vesta Tilley was permitted to represent the respectable face of Music Hall and Ellen Terry was allowed to have the 'common touch' precisely because she was so uncommon. Ellen Terry and Vesta Tilley were exceptions, and by their careful presentation as such effectively reinforced the whole caste system. Most women on either side of the great divide between the Music Hall artiste and the artist of serious drama — which was very clearly a class division — were untouched by the space that both these two women created for themselves. In fact the allowing of the occasional 'special case', labelled as the privilege and reward of 'genius', further insured the whole caste system. In the last analysis, neither Ellen Terry nor Vesta Tilley ever seriously tried to challenge the conventions, but rather, they skilfully and successfully manipulated them to their own individual advantage.

Despite all this it was real kudos for Vesta Tilley to have Ellen Terry on her own stage (or rather, Oswald Stoll's) saying, in the voice that had thrilled thousands,

I am not going to make a speech. I could not say enough of what I think of this wonderful little lady [neither the adjectives nor the noun are without significance] . . . I know this: that if I do begin to speak I shall never leave off. Miss Tilley does not know what she has done for England. She has made us laugh when — God knows — we needed to laugh. Now she deserves a crown, but I have not got a crown about me. So I will present her with a palm.[13]

Vesta Tilley, after this touching speech, 'laid her head on Ellen Terry's shoulder and wept'. Before we are too moved by this touching, and highly self-conscious vignette we must recall Vesta Tilley's own extreme care for her 'respectable' self-presentation. She had been careful; she never wore drag offstage, not even to theatrical fancy-dress parties; she demonstrated her love of feminine frills, and particularly for jewellery, whenever possible; she refused — at first sight an improbable lapse of her vaunted professionalism — to cut her hair. She emphasized her own 'professionalism' and purity in every way she could. In her *Recollections* she goes out of her way to relate how totally absorbed in her artistic career she was, even as an adolescent on the road, and how strictly her father had chaperoned her. The only glamour in her life, she was to insist, was 'the glamour of the evening when I took my place behind the kerosene footlights', and she made great efforts to distinguish between the moral virtue of the true professional and the vulgarity of other performers:

In my long experience I do not think I have ever met a girl who was serious in her intention to devote her talent to the entertainment of the public, who had the time or inclination to gad about with titled nonentities, turn night into day and generally lead the public to believe that the life of an actress was one long round of pleasure and excitement with notoriety as the biggest asset. On the contrary, those who by dint of hard work and ability carved out a position for themselves reaped their reward by the time they kept their position as public favourites and the domestic happiness they achieved in their retirement after years of hard work . . . whilst more often than not, the girl who leaps suddenly into notoriety by some accident of fate or deliberate intent, soon disappears from public view and unfortunately often ends life in distressing circumstances. The publicity given to the exciting life of these shooting stars naturally leads those of the public who are interested to imagine that an actress's life is not all it should be from the moral and domestic point of view . . . If I moralise it is because I love my profession and it hurts me to see the publicity given to so many girls who have not the slightest claim to the title of actress and whose behaviour casts a slur on an honoured profession.[14]

Vesta Tilley sounds here like every other Victorian middle-class Mrs Grundy. Her moralism is not so much a deep-rooted purity of soul as a dread of being branded, like other Music Hall artistes, as less than 'artistic', and therefore less than respectable, less than bourgeois.

Yet Vesta Tilley's profound yearning for respectability has to be set in its own context. She had spent over fifty years in professional Music Hall and she knew only too well the havoc that it wreaked in many women's personal lives. Bessie Bellwood, the first 'Queen of the Halls', died in 1896, aged only thirty-nine. If anyone should have been a survivor it was she. Born in Northern Ireland and brought up in Bermond-sey, London, where she worked as a child skinning rabbits,

she was tough and aggressive in her own interests. Her début
was described thus:

She was at once heckled by a hefty-looking coal-heaver who made it
clear he had no intention of allowing his drinking to be disturbed. A
slanging match ensued with Bessie declaring her intention of 'wiping
down the bloomin' hall with him and making it respectable.' For
over five minutes she let fly, leaving him gasping, dazed and
speechless. At the end, she gathered herself together for one supreme
effort and hurled him an insult so bitter with scorn, so sharp with
insight into his career and character, so heavy with prophetic curse,
that strong men drew and held their breath while it passed over
them and women hid their faces and shivered.[15]

But this instinct for self-survival, the warmth and practical
generosity for which she was famed, and the adoration of her
fans could not protect her. Her most popular song, 'Wot
Cheer Ria', had demonstrated her awareness of the dangers in
trying to rise out of the class to which you belong, and she
never attempted what Vesta Tilley was to pull off; exhaustion
and drink killed her.

Vesta Tilley's own early idol, Nellie Power, to whom she
had been content to play 'Second Boy' in the Drury Lane
Pantomime of 1882, also died in poverty and ill-health before
her thirtieth birthday. Jennie Hill, perhaps the other greatest
star of the first generation of Music Hall women, was forty-
four when she died, but she had been unable to perform for
the last ten years of her life because her health had been so
frail.

The women of Vesta Tilley's own generation fared little
better. Only the lives of the stars are recorded, so it is
impossible to know what happened to the mass of women
who were not even sufficiently successful to be remembered.
But Lottie Collins, an exact contemporary of Vesta Tilley's,
and with whom she formed as near as she ever came to a close
female friendship, died in 1910 at the age of forty-four. Her
life had been marked by chaos and unhappiness. She first rose

to stardom with the still-famous song, 'Ta-ra-ra-boom-de-ay', with its catchy tune and bizarre presentation:

Starting on rather a demure note, she would pause at the end of the verse, place her hand defiantly on her hip and whirl into a furious high-kicking apache can-can dance which sent audiences wild and often left Lottie fainting in the wings . . . It caused a sensation, in which accusations from the purity league were mixed with the bravos of music hall audiences and did much to establish the reputation of the so-called 'Naughty Nineties'.[16]

The physical rigours of her act and her almost obsessive need to meet the demands of the audiences for encores and repeat performances probably broke her health: there are agonizing accounts of her being unable to leave the stage at the end of a performance. But reputation and expectation obviously caught up with her too, because she was married three times and scandal followed her career.

Vesta Tilley's most obvious rival at the top of the popularity charts — and hence the wage structure, although Vesta Tilley was consistently better at getting good contracts — was, of course, Marie Lloyd. She at least survived into her fifties, but was punished severely by society for her complete refusal to cooperate in any way with the necessary conventions of hypocrisy. Apart from her three divorces, which she managed to make more public by living openly with her new lovers before she received her decrees, she chose a warned-off jockey for one of her husbands. When she visited America in 1913 she was arrested and incarcerated on Ellis Island for 'moral turpitude' because she and her lover had shared a cabin on the journey — and she *had told journalists this* when they had asked her. She died poor and sad in 1922.

Vesta Tilley must have been frightened by what she saw: Lottie Collins ostracized and dead; Marie Lloyd making more headlines for her sex life than for her enormous talent. Moreover, she lacked the strong family bond that Marie Lloyd had with her sisters, and must have feared emotional isolation. She knew too that these women were the elite;

below them was a great mass of hungry, poor, desperate women, whom society ignored when it did not insult, and whose profession was regarded as coterminous with prostitution, to which, doubtless, many did in fact turn. The lot of most working-class women, especially during the economic depression of the 1870s and 1880s, was unenviable; but failed Music Hall singers were regarded as being outside the pale of society altogether.

Vesta Tilley must have been additionally wary because her own act was potentially dubious on so many levels. Apart from the danger of being associated with sexual immorality, she also ran the risk of being stigmatized as a freak. Many of the most popular acts of Music Hall were exotic, or nourished by the old fascination with the freak. Chang and Eng, the original Siamese Twins, made their living in Vaudeville, as did the poor, gentle Robert Waldow, billed as 'The Tallest Man Who Ever Lived'. Music Hall was filled with acts, usually described as 'Exotics', whose fame was based on their presentation of personal peculiarity, ranging from the fascination with orientalism, through acrobatics, down to the crudely 'pseudo-scientific'. In 1893 'Athleta', a woman gymnast and weight-lifter, had a very successful season in London, billed as 'The Strongest Woman in the World'. Hypnotists, mindreaders, magicians, physical oddities and scientific demonstrators also flourished, bringing to Music Hall some of the raffish atmosphere of the travelling shows, circuses and freak shows which they had displaced. One of the most popular of the freak-show presentations was the 'hermaphrodite', the man/woman of myth. By the nineteenth century the presentation of these androgynes had moved away from the seventeenth- and eighteenth-century genital display and was more concerned with presenting the social side of gender confusion:

Such human enigmas are decked out on one side in what fashion decreed as male garb and on the other on what was accepted as female . . . Before unisex clothes and hairstyling even such superficial counterfeits of androgyny seem to have provided audiences with sufficient thrill, though there were always those who wanted to see more and were willing to pay to see the 'morphodites' strip down . . . Some fairground Hermaphrodites must have been true intersexes, freaky enough to satisfy any beholder; but most in all probability were fakes, just trying to make a living, or responding to a psychic dissatisfaction with their physiological gender.[17]

Contemporaneous with Vesta Tilley, some of these performers were still achieving considerable popularity, especially in the cheaper Halls and in the circuses. They were usually presented under double names, and with publicity material that stressed the oddness and the 'scientific' interest that they could offer to the spectator: the sexual aspect always hidden discreetly under high Music Hall verbiage. The most successful of these was certainly Josephine/Joseph who toured internationally under expert management.

Although there was a sufficient tradition within the acting profession of impersonation and 'breeches parts' to give some credit to Vesta Tilley's artistic claims, the better her art was — the nearer it came to raising questions about 'natural gender' — the more she must have felt threatened by this other aspect of presentation in the Music Hall. Most Music Hall *aficionados* have been very silent about this aspect of the Halls, though one previewer of the Royal Command Performance heaved a sigh of relief when he remarked that all animal and 'sensation' acts had been omitted, in the name of good taste. But for Vesta Tilley it must have been a spectre of fear, and one more reason why in public she was so careful always to appear as the womanly woman, neat, pretty, beautifully and ornamentally dressed, generous to children and tender towards her loving husband.

It was her work as a performer which made her escape from her working-class background possible, at the same time that work made it particularly hard for her to enter fully into the social milieu she craved. The whole role of the actress and what she represented in society was, for working-class women, a complex double bind. Vesta Tilley found her way through this tricky opening, but inevitably this increasingly isolated her from her women colleagues; she felt obliged to stress her own uniqueness: her own womanliness, her own ladylikeness, in contrast to all the others. Her enterprise was a high risk one; she could not have afforded, either emotionally or financially, a single lapse from grace, nor too many gestures of real solidarity with her less privileged sisters.

THE WOMAN DRAG ARTIST

> Her modesty as to her writing, her vanity as to her person, her fears for her safety, all seem to hint what was said a short time ago about there being no change in Orlando the man and Orlando the woman, was ceasing to be altogether true. She was becoming a little more modest, as women are, of her brains, and a little more vain, as women are, of her person. Certain susceptibilities were asserting themselves, and others were diminishing. The change of clothes had, some philosophers will say, much to do with it. Vain trifles as they seem, clothes have they say, more important offices than merely to keep us warm. They change our view of the world and the world's view of us.
>
> *Virginia Woolf* [1]

> Transvestism becomes the active verb in a sentence of self-obliteration.
>
> *Marina Warner* [2]

There are at least four reasons, it seems, why women in fiction and myth and history dress up as men. Firstly, and apparently simply, they may do it for disguise: for whatever reason a woman wishes, or needs, to be perceived as, treated as, and believed to be a man. In the vocabulary of transsexualism, she wants to 'pass' in the social world as a member of the other gender: her most important, basic act is to put on men's clothes. For motives ranging from the pathological to the pragmatic, women choose to appear as men for anything from a few hours to their whole life span.

It is hard to enumerate the instances, because only the failures get found out and so recorded, but there are a number of cases of women who have passed as men successfully for very long periods or even for the whole of their lives. 'James Barry', for instance, was born in 1799 and by the age of ten had disguised her original gender identity sufficiently well to become a medical student at Edinburgh University. She became a doctor, enlisted in the army and in 1822 became a colonial medical officer; for the next forty years she worked within the Colonial Service in widely flung corners of the British Empire, including Canada, Corfu, Malta and the Leeward and Windward Islands. Her biological gender was not discovered until after her death in 1865.

Mary Anne Talbot, born in 1778, lived for most of her life as a sailor named 'James Taylor' and was so successful that 'she actually made a conquest of the Captain's niece . . . the young lady even went so far as to propose marriage.' Mary Talbot was 'exposed', but although she returned to England to live as a woman, she 'could not so far forget my sea-faring habits, but frequently dressed myself and took excursions as a sailor.'[3]

There is, of course, a much larger group of women who dressed up as men for briefer periods of time. Literature, folklore, medieval hagiography and mythology are full of women who, often in order to escape sexual harassment or to be able to travel more freely, disguised themselves as men. Shakespeare's heroines, Viola and Rosalind, are perhaps the best-known of the more modern fictional examples, while Portia's costume of a lawyer enabled her to perform a 'professional' role impossible for a woman. But verifiable historical accounts also exist from all generations. Jessie Kenney, Vesta Tilley's contemporary, used to dress up as a messenger boy to carry instructions from Christabel Pankhurst in Paris to the militant suffragists in London: not only was she entirely successful, but the escapade was obviously a source of pride and amusement to her fellow suffragettes who took photographs of her in the streets in London. Ethel le Neve, Dr Crippen's mistress, disguised herself as his son during their abortive escape attempt after his murder of his wife. The disguise in this instance was a notable failure, but this was largely due to the couple's indiscretion: it was the sight of the 'father' and 'son' in a passionate embrace that first alerted the ship's captain to the truth of the couple's identity.

Ethel le Neve was an exception: despite the ideological conviction that women and men are of totally different physical types, many of these disguises succeeded entirely in their aim (as did the reverse: Bonnie Prince Charlie, as the most wanted man in Britain, really did escape disguised as Flora MacDonald's maid). By and large, women seem to have assumed these disguises to transcend the limits imposed upon them: it was impossible to be a woman doctor, woman sailor, or woman soldier in the societies in which these women were making choices (although it is interesting to note that women still assume at least a partial 'disguise' if they want to perform roles that are still regarded as 'male': women soldiers and women businessmen both present themselves in masculinized attire beyond the point of convenience or necessity). Although they did not make thoroughgoing attempts to disguise their gender, women like Ann Bonny, Mary Read and Anne Mills − three eighteenth-century women convicted of piracy − always wore men's clothes and did so clearly in order to equate themselves with men in a male-dominated community. Thérèse Figueur (1774−1861) became a soldier in the French Revolutionary Army; although she never tried to lose her biological gender, she was discreet about it, always wore full uniform and was explicit about the effects that this had on her personal life:

After that [her decision to don a uniform] I could go about with my uncle anywhere, even on campaign. Nature in a jesting mood had caused me to be born a woman. I now returned that quip.[4]

Although her comrades knew of the 'imposture' they do not seem to have objected and she fought alongside them throughout the French revolutionary wars and was personally decorated by Napoleon.

Although the personal consequences for the women who undertook this solution to their entrapment within gender expectations were not uniformly happy, such women seem to have excited surprisingly little, truly vicious opprobrium so long as they did not try to go 'too far'. As Peter Ackroyd says:

Such activities were characteristically seen as ambitious rather than degrading, an attempt to be 'as good' as men. Of course female transvestism would become unsettling if large numbers of women were engaged in it (hence the persistence of Amazon myths) but it has generally been treated as a harmless and somehow aesthetically pleasing eccentricity. It is not as threatening as male-transvestism, and this unacknowledged sexism is a major element in all forms of 'acceptable' transvestism: female cross-dressing actually enhances the putative superiority of male culture.[5]

It is important though to remember that this 'aesthetically pleasing eccentricity' must, according to the 'laws' of a sexist society, be treated as a privilege generously bestowed upon some women, and not as the right of any 'bold' woman. Mandy Merck, for example, has argued persuasively that the persistence of Amazon myths does not celebrate the power of women to transcend gender limitations so much as the power of men to overcome and defeat all women who attempt such transcendence or create cultures that challenge male 'civilizations' – all Amazon figures are finally killed by, or subjugated through love of the heroic male.[6] Similarly, when Thérèse Figueur was captured with her companions-at-arms of several years and long campaigns in the Piedmont, the local community demanded that she be handed over to be burned as a witch (dressing in men's clothes was one of the signs of being a witch); her fellow soldiers made absolutely no protest and she escaped burning only through her own ingenuity. Her privileges were withdrawn promptly under the smallest pressure. None the less, Ackroyd's definition seems to hold

Vesta Tilley. Publicity postcards

Vesta Tilley, principal boy,
aged 14

Walter de Frece with Vesta Tilley.
Publicity postcard

Dan Leno – Pantomime Dame.
Publicity picture

Nelly Power – an early Music Hall
Impersonator

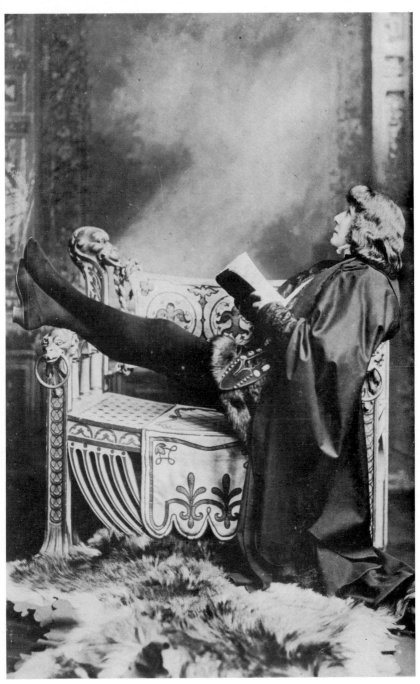

Sarah Bernhardt as 'Hamlet'. Publicity postcard

Colette in drag

Beatrice Lillie in revue

Jessie Kenney disguised

The suffragette Elsie James as Joan of Arc

Marlene Dietrich in 'Morocco'

Greta Garbo as 'Queen Christina'

Josephine/Joseph – 'Freak hermaphrodite'. Publicity picture

George Sand

Above: 'The Modern Girl' – anti-feminist cartoon, 1898

Left: 'Mary Hamilton' – line drawing by Toulouse Lautrec

true at least about 'disguise' cross-dressing: the decision to identify visually with dominant 'maleness' is perceived as a (justifiable) criticism of one's own (naturally) limited femaleness, and is therefore at least partially pleasing to the dominant culture — provided, of course, that it is not excessive, and does not include claims to male sex objects.

A second reason for women to adopt men's clothes is sexual. In some cases this is an overt and public statement of object choice — many lesbians, particularly in the first half of this century, used men's clothes: Radclyffe Hall, Colette, and a number of the early lesbian night-club acts of the 1920s and 1930s, particularly in Paris and Berlin, used male costume as a way of publicly declaring their sexual choice. In some earlier examples, which might superficially belong to the category of 'disguise', it seems evident that the women were gay and dressed as men principally in order to 'explain' their own preference. Molly Hamilton, the true-life 'heroine' of Henry Fielding's *The Female Husband* (1746) adopted male dress after a homosexual relationship, and subsequently went so far as to marry women on three different occasions. She was finally flogged and imprisoned — and certainly did not receive the privileges of 'eccentricity'. Fielding concluded: 'It is to be hoped that this example will be sufficient to deter all others from the commission of such foul and unnatural crimes.' (*The Female Husband* is a singularly unattractive work: a nasty mixture of male prurience and mysogynistic moralism.) Although contemporary lesbian feminism has rightly come to be critical of the role-playing and male identification involved in male-impersonation, it may still be seen as a courageous decision for individual women in a very difficult, and different, historical context.

However, it would be a mistake to make a simplistic association between wearing men's clothes and female homosexuality. The evidence that wearing items of women's clothing, often in secret, is sexually arousing to men is incontrovertible, and patently not associated with homosexuality. The problem in trying to decide how much, if at all, this works in reverse for women is that there is so little female erotica available. Pornography is a male product, designed for and consumed by men, totally unconcerned with female sexual arousal, but only with women as male fantasy objects. There is, inevitably, pornography in which women are shown wearing men's clothes; but these images offer no reliable information as to whether or not women do gain any erotic pleasure from dressing-up as men − donning Y-fronts, for example, or dressing up as soldiers, clergymen or prize-fighters.

Apart from male fantasies, there is a political element in the presentation of women in this area that further complicates the issue. Early feminism was often − as contemporary feminism still is − presented as an 'unnatural' attempt, springing from sexual pathology, by women to imitate men through *clothing*. The role of clothing in the representation of feminism, from Bloomers to Bra-burning, as the way in which a hostile media could best present the idiocy and the danger of feminism is fascinating. This obsession with what feminists *wear* is perhaps no more than a desperate attempt to reduce feminism to the most 'superficial' level possible, and thus to trivialize it. Because of the complex nature of cultural male dominance and the power to control images of women and of sexuality, available for 'public' consumption, it is very difficult to assess the role that drag does, or could, play in women's independent sexuality.

The third reason for male-impersonation is religious. Here mythology and practice become deeply entwined; many religions have used 'feasts of reversal' or individual mythological figures, ritually represented, in various ways. This ritualizing of difference in order both to contain and to defuse it is by no means confined to gender difference. Ancient Egyptian court religion, for example, had an elaborate ritual dance in which priests mimicked dwarfs and other forms of 'deformity' in order to placate the mystery contained therein. But gender difference and gender confusion, along with matters of fertility and death, were central to the concerns of religious ritual across many cultures. Bearded women, hermaphroditic gods, Teiresias figures and other motifs of this sort crop up almost universally and are frequently accompanied by ritual acting-out of the confusion. For instance, there are many themes of deceiving the spirits by men dressing as women before battle, or women dressing as men before childbirth in order to ward off gender-specific dangers. However, the idea of male superiority and the male control of religion has meant that men usually have more access to these 'passing over' rituals than women do. There are a great number of shamanistic cults in which the male shaman goes into 'the world of women' to acquire additional knowledge and wisdom, but far fewer examples in which this happens in reverse.

Because Western drama has evolved out of religious and ritual representations, the connection here is important. Popular British Pantomime indeed sprang originally from the Roman feast of Saturnalia, a major feast of social reversal: women dressed as men, men as women, slaves and their owners swapped roles; hence the origins not only of the Principal Boy and the Dame, but also of elements like the traditional poverty of the nobility in Pantomime — where kings inhabit palaces called 'Stoneybroke Castle' and noble barons are forced to borrow cash from their servants. Christianity, partly because it sprang from that most practical and least ritualistic of all religions, Judaism, and partly because of its unique desire for an all-male deity, always expressed an extreme fear of gender confusion. None the less, it failed to eliminate altogether the remnants of such feasts. Holy Innocents, the Feast of Fools and the spring festivals associated with mummery were maintained throughout Europe well into this century: all of these involved social reversal, including gender impersonation, and were usually accompanied by considerable sexual licence. Mardi Gras is now perhaps the last of these feasts, and it is well-known for its tolerance of drag.

In Europe since the seventeenth century, rationalism in

thought and social realism in representation have increasingly dominated the cultural media and have driven out ritual and magic. There is little, if any, consciousness of the ritualistic aspects of gender impersonation. By the nineteenth century confusion over gender identity was socially 'outlawed' – even clothes were designed to accentuate the unbridgeable gulf between the sexes. Ambivalence was driven underground and obliged to take expression in sexual deviance and 'antisocial' conduct, while ancient questions and doubts were declared illegitimate. None the less, the ritualistic aspects of gender impersonation are worth describing because so many of our contemporary cultural forms – as Pantomime demonstrates – have evolved out of Christian and pre-Christian religious practices.

All three reasons for women dressing in men's clothes need to be kept in mind as we look at the fourth, and the one most central to this book, performance drag. By this I mean the idea that a woman assumes male clothes in order to play with – at whatever level of consciousness – ideas about gender in relationship with an 'audience'. This is radically different from the concept of disguise, since it is a primary necessity of all 'impersonation' that the audience should be aware that it *is* an impersonation. The audience response may include an element of wonder and fascination at the conviction that the impersonation carries; there is never room for error, or even for serious doubt or speculation. Hence the wisdom of Vesta Tilley's London manager who insisted in the early days that she change her stage name lest there be any doubt or confusion about her 'real' or 'natural' gender.

There is very little contemporary material which treats performance drag for what it is: although there may well be personal or psychological reasons why an individual artist should adopt this particular type of act, it is unhelpful to treat performance drag as a 'psychopathological' symptom since the act can only exist when there is an audience, a society, which understands gender difference clearly enough to get the joke. Performance drag is a socio-cultural event. Crudely, a society that did not use the manipulation of external appearance (through clothing, body paint, hair-arrangement) as a code to sexual difference, or indeed a society that had no concept of gender difference as a social determinant could not be interested in impersonation. If 'unisex' appearance were a reality, representing a genuine lack of interest in gender difference, there would be no place for gender impersonation. Conversely, a society which was psychically and sexually confident in an absolute divide between one gender and the other could not experience impersonation as interesting, because the idea of ambivalence would be meaningless and therefore without performance value.

Neither of these extremes is the case in our society, nor, as far as I know, in any society of which we have historical records. However, different phases of society have put different meanings on gender difference, and perceived different values in its representation: obviously, then, the meaning of cross-gender impersonation in performance is not fixed, but reflects quite subtly the real role of gender difference in different cultural communities.

It is important to bear in mind that the field of gender impersonation is dominated and controlled by men, and therefore usually informed by male understandings of female sexuality. A woman impersonating a man, if she is careful, can seem 'ambitious', and even 'misplaced' ambition is not a totally negative quality. She may have 'ideas above her station' but she is at least aiming for the heights. She can be indulged – just as the tomboy is indulged. But for a man to impersonate a woman is for him to undertake, voluntarily, an act of self-humiliation (unless he can make the woman sufficiently ridiculous for his identification with 'her' to be seen as absurd). As one male drag artist put it, when asked if there were any 'straight' (non-homosexual) female-impersonators: 'in practice there may be a few, but in theory there can't be any. How could you do this work and not have something wrong with you?'[7]

Within the male gay community there is some 'glamour

drag' — an attempt to represent genuinely 'beautiful' women, although always of a beauty consonant with male standards. Most female-impersonation — and any which is allowed mass appeal — caricatures the least attractive female stereotypes, the crone (in Pantomime), the repressed spinster (Hinge and Brackett), or the self-deluding, vulgar, loudmouth (Dame Edna Everage, or Pantomime's Ugly Sisters). Meanwhile, male-impersonators usually present favourable images of masculinity: the hero — be he soldier, Pantomime prince or dandy; the beautiful young man, whose decadence can even be charming; or the dashing drunk, not the down-at-heel wino. The response to popular female-impersonation is hilarity; to popular male-impersonation it is a sort of sentimental kindliness or an unfocused sexual curiosity.

But this is simply a social response, a socially-constructed attitude towards a specific genre of performance. It has not always been so. Performance drag in ritual settings can produce awe and veneration in certain cultures. Japanese theatrical tradition produces a form of female-impersonation which is neither ludicrous nor naturalistic. The male Kabuki players and *onnagata* essentially do 'straight drag', despite the fact that their cultural background is as oppressive to women as Western culture. In the Western cultural tradition, opera has men — originally castrati — playing women's roles and women playing men's roles (the title role in *Xerxes* for instance) without ridicule.

Goethe saw this heightening of artifice in opera as a significant benefit:

Thus a double pleasure is given in that these persons are not women but only represent women. The young men have studied the properties of the sex in its being and behaviour; they know them thoroughly and reproduce them like an artist; they represent not themselves, but a nature absolutely foreign to them.[8]

The complex gender confusions of Shakespearean comedy, where men play women playing men, present new and hopeful possibilities rather than an occasion for rib-poking hilarity. Often, as in *Twelfth Night*, the gender confusion is neither criticized nor fully resolved — the introduction of the 'twin' means that the 'mistake' that Olivia makes in her choice of love-object is actually condoned and encouraged. Oscar Wilde, himself an active proponent of gender confusion, wrote about these characters with deep delight:

Shakespeare does not merely disguise his characters; he transforms them. The influence of the costume penetrates to the very soul of the wearer . . . But these beings of indefinite sex — how are we to regard them save as angels or fairies? . . . They are the kin of Ariel, that multiform spirit.[9]

Roland Barthes, in his book *The Pleasures of the Text*, draws a distinction between the pleasure of resolution offered by the classical text and the 'bliss' which comes from a text that denies a final resolution.[10] This experience of new openings, of non-resolution, is simply not available in any modern forms of gender impersonation, which always offer the 'consolation' of absolute resolution: at the end of the performance the absolute 'reality' of gender roles is affirmed. And so is their social meaning — maleness is superior to femaleness, but at the same time there is no escape from biological destiny. The 'bliss' of real ambivalence is avoided.

Perhaps a good example of this insistence on resolution is seen in the film *Tootsie*, where Dustin Hoffman, for non-sexual narrative motives, dresses up as a woman to the confusion of the other characters in the film.[11] Despite a very impressive and sympathetic performance by Dustin Hoffman, the audience is never confused — we are let in on the ground floor, as it were, and see every detail of how the trick is worked. We are never confused, our assumptions about gender are never put at risk. Our curiosity is ultimately vicarious — we may want to know how the plot will be resolved, how people will feel when they are finally un-deceived, but we are safe, not deceived for an instant. We are allowed to know that we are more knowing, that we are nearer the truth than the characters in the film, and this is the source of our satisfaction and our amusement.

I do not know any performance representation that exposes the audience to the risk of real gender confusion and the possibility of Barthes's 'bliss'. This does happen occasionally in other art forms – in Aubrey Beardsley's drawings, in Virginia Woolf's *Orlando* (1928) or in Théophile Gautier's *Mademoiselle de Maupin* (1835), for example. But the final refusal to put the audience at risk seems to characterize all recent performance drag, and obliges it, formally, to remain at the level of slapstick or titillation.

In her article, *Sexual Disguise and Cinema*, the contemporary feminist critic Annette Kuhn suggests that in our society there is a real dilemma within performance drag.[12] On the one hand, performing, acting, is something which necessarily 'involves pretence dissimulation and intent to seem to be something you are, in reality, not. An actor's role is assumed like a mask . . . concealing the "true" self.' On the other hand, our culture teaches us that gender is fixed and absolute; 'it lies at the heart of human subjectivity' and so it is something that necessarily *cannot* be pretended or assumed. The very enterprise of performance drag is therefore inherently contradictory. Out of this contradiction it ought to be possible for a very complex range of emotions to be built up. For the great male-impersonators this has always been the intention; but our society is weighted against such complexity, particularly in cases where it might favour the real advancement of women. Indeed the fear of this complexity may explain why gender impersonation has so often been tabooed, outlawed, or firmly associated with sexual deviance.

Nevertheless, against the odds, there has been a sequence of great male-impersonators. It is important to remember that these performances are not necessarily 'theatrical' in the strict sense of that word; the male-impersonators use men's clothes in front of audiences (which may be as large as their whole social world) to make political or social points, and to exploit sexual ambivalence to their own advantage. These are not women who are driven by anxiety or guilt about their desire to wear men's clothes; not for them the sad ejaculation of Mary Frith, for example, who felt literally driven by her own 'perverse' desires:

I beheld myself more obnoxious to my Fate; and have a greater quarrel with that, than the world can have against me. It was my Fate not me; I do more wonder at myself than others can do . . . I see myself so wholly distempered and so estranged as if I had been born and bred in the Antipodes.[13]

The male-impersonators had a vast range of 'stages' and of intentions, but a tradition does bind these women together. They all impersonated the 'beau idéal' of their own societies − the soldier, the artist, the dandy and, most recently, the androgyne. They were all aping the male norm that was also the male aspiration. Perhaps the greatest of them all was Joan of Arc (1412−31). Marina Warner, in her book *Joan of Arc*, makes clear the importance which Joan's knightly costume had, not only for her personally, but for the society in which she was trying to live.[14] Warner emphasizes that Joan was not trying *to disguise* herself as a man. She always called herself not 'Joan of Arc' as we do now, but a more explicitly female title, 'Jeanne La Pucelle', Joan the Maid. She was trying to create a middle ground, a gender-free space in which she might be free to achieve the complex task to which she felt herself divinely called. She, like Vesta Tilley, laboured under a double disadvantage: not only was she the 'wrong' gender, she was also, as absolutely, the wrong class. Her self-appointed role was to be the knightly hero, the '*chevalier d'honneur sans peur et sans reproche*' − the obvious hero for a feudal society engaged in an interminable, heroic war. She was also in pursuit of Christian virtue: the word itself is associated with masculinity, since it comes from the Latin *vir* − a man. By insisting on wearing men's clothes − and not just men's, but *noblemen's* − she was attempting to enter a new sphere, one available in her culture if not in ours, the a-material sphere of heaven.

Through her transvestism, she abrogated the destiny of womankind. She could thereby transcend her sex; she could set herself apart and usurp the privileges of the male and his claims to superiority. At the same time, by never pretending to be other than a woman and a maid, she was usurping a man's function but shaking off the trammels of his sex altogether to occupy a different, third order, neither male nor female, but unearthly, like the angels whose company she loved.[15]

During her brief career Joan's 'performance' was more total than that of most male-impersonators. But her life does have certain parallels with later impersonators, in particular, with Vesta Tilley: for example, Joan's insistence, in all matters other than dress, on a rigorous sexual respectability. For the fifteenth century this meant virginity, for Vesta Tilley it meant marriage, but both of them placed an extremely high value on their own purity, manifested as sexual conformity. The form of their chastities was different, but for both of them the risks involved in presuming to dress as men were off-set by a disciplined and evangelical purity. Both of them used the externals of maleness to achieve 'upward mobility', but both of them also seemed to have recognized instinctively that there was a price to be paid for acceptance into the world of masculinity. Abstinence was in the fifteenth century what wifeliness was in the nineteenth (and what heterosexual activity is in the late twentieth): the clear sign of the 'good woman'. (Marlene Dietrich's well publicized 'happy marriage', and Annie Lennox' well publicized failed marriage are also of course part of this same complex.) Both of them were child-free, and both of them were physically 'under-developed': Joan's amenorrhoea was used as 'evidence' both by her supporters and detractors, to emphasize her asexuality. Vesta Tilley, in an age of swelling bosoms and lavish flesh, maintained a weight of under seven stone and 'as trim a figure as most people have ever seen'.

Queen Christina of Sweden's life presents different questions. Having abdicated her throne in 1654, she adopted a man's name as well as male clothing and at one stage was known as Count Dohna, but this clearly did not fully fit her own image of herself as 'special'. Brought up to the throne of Sweden, she had a childhood that had prepared her for exclusive privilege, and queens themselves, though not unheard of, were in some senses sufficiently rare to command a special status – a status, it should be born in mind, that they used very frequently either for pathos or for power. Christina quickly found that travelling as a Swedish count was a 'pleasing eccentricity' which the courts of Europe were quite prepared to tolerate, at least in an ex-monarch and a well-heeled one at that. It was only when she reverted to her own name and to a confusing and uneasy amalgam of male and female costume that she became the great 'performance event' of courtly Europe. There were other highly dramatized events in her subsequent career. Her attempts to get her throne back and her loudly trumpeted conversion to Roman Catholicism both created international scandal – but it was her cross-dressing, the exoticism of her public sexual ambivalence, that made all her actions so exciting to her 'audience'. Christina did not need to use maleness to achieve upward social mobility like Joan of Arc and Vesta Tilley; nor did she need the social protection of sexual respectability, but the desire for autonomy and independence from the pressures of her family and from social conventions were present in her life, as much as theirs. Her provocative use of her own privileges exposes the complexity of class and gender oppression. She wanted to make a clear and public statement about her own gender, her own life choices and she found that male-impersonation gained her more attention – a larger audience – than male disguise.

George Sand, the pen name and chosen persona of Amantine Lucile Aurore Daupin, Baronne Dudevant, was born in 1804. She deserted her noble husband in 1831 and became as famous for her sexual adventures with eminent members of the artistic world, like Chopin and Alfred de Musset, as she did for her writings, which were often

intensely 'romantic'. Her career showed an interesting development from being a propagandist of free love for women
equally with men, through her political involvement with a
broad range of humanitarian reform movements, and finally to
her retreat into rural life, when she wrote studies of nature
and rustic life-styles. For George Sand, the adoption of men's
clothes was meant to signal a deliberate break not only with
the social constrictions imposed upon women, but with the
whole concept of the social order itself. Her early novels like
Indiana (1832), and *Lélia* (1833) suggest how strong the
notion of chaos, or anarchy, was for her in her fight for freer
sexual expression.[16] George Sand, by dressing in men's
clothing, was directly challenging the rationalism of the post-
Renaissance, through sexually irrational and therefore 'unnatural' conduct. Her performance was part of a literary
movement: her decade of cross-dressing (the 1830s) also saw
the publication of Théophile Gautier's *Mademoiselle de Maupin*
(1835), an extraordinary novel about sexual reversals of an
extremely troubling kind. The novel addresses the question of
the social construction of gender through clothes and life-
styles, as well as through sexual object choice. Gautier
examines how cross-dressing creates new possibilities of
perception by throwing into confusion the certainties of
'natural' gender-role. His narrator, confronted with the cross-
dressed heroine, comes to doubt his own sexual nature:

I no longer feel certain who I am or what others are . . . I feel as
utterly isolated as anyone can be, and all the links between myself
and external objects and between external objects and myself have
been broken one by one.

But through this experience of alienation there is space for a
new growth: 'I comprehend many many things which I never
used to comprehend, I perceive amazing affinities for the first
time.'

In a cultural climate receptive to the literary potential of
such ideas, George Sand attempted to use sexual ambivalence
to create a personal freedom. But there is a crucial difference

between literature and reality: the 'Third Sex' that she sought to join simply does not exist; women are obliged to 'pretend' to certain qualities of masculinity in order to achieve personal freedoms. These freedoms will inevitably be granted only to a limited number of women who will present them in a socially controllable way. The Romantic movement isolated artists precisely by separating them from the 'common mould'; they were allowed to 'get away' with personal peculiarities (drunkenness, drug abuse, sexual libertarianism and absent-mindedness being among the favoured eccentricities) to a considerable extent, but paid the price for this privilege in being exiled from common experience. In this way the artist can, in terms of her representation, indeed become 'androgynous', as Virginia Woolf recommended, precisely because she is exempted from the material laws which affect 'ordinary people'. At the same time, however, the potential challenge to wider, societal norms is vitiated by presenting such 'special privilege' as precisely that − both the rewards and the price of genius, an uncontrollable, random, bolt-from-the-blue. In many ways George Sand did create for herself an individual freedom greater than that enjoyed by many women, but her subsequent retreat from politics into arcadianism is not surprising; and her life was treated as a Work of Art, an artificial fiction, more interesting even than her own work. For women artists, sexuality still remains a deflection from, rather than an enhancement of, their serious work.

During the nineteenth century such endeavours became more difficult. Middle-class women were increasingly confined to the home and therefore lacked an audience, in the social sense, to respond to the conflicting images of gender. Their forays out tended to be in 'higher causes' which could not be put at risk by raising questions of sexuality. Amelia Bloomer's well thought-out attack on the gender division in dress codes floundered in the 1850s under the weight of the mockery it attracted, although in both Britain and America her Rational Dress Society originally attracted considerable support.

Costume had become a very important sign of social gender, and social gender was completely absorbed at this time into the idea of 'natural gender'. The only space for cross-dressing had to be within the realms of the artificial. At the same time the growth of the entertainment industry, for both middle- and working-class audiences, provided a new arena for gender impersonation. By the end of the century performance drag in England was almost entirely confined to the stage. But there at least it became acceptable. At the 'higher' end of the cultural spectrum, the performing of men's roles became the ultimate artistic challenge for the ambitious, serious actress: Sarah Bernhardt's Hamlet of 1900 is perhaps the most famous and successful of these endeavours, but she was working within an established tradition. At the beginning of the century Madame Vestris and Mrs Howard Paul were both presenting 'breeches parts' to some consternation — the *Morning Chronicle* complained in 1829 that Madame Vestris chose 'the very tightest buckskins she could obtain to fit her shape'. The classical actress Ellen Tree, rather more decorously clad, as the century advanced, played Romeo. Women also regularly played boys and young men's parts, and perhaps not surprisingly, the characters of subnormal or effete men and youths. The great actor-manager Macready, who cast a teenage girl, Pricilla Horton, as the Fool in his production of *King Lear*, summed up the ideal for this part as a 'fragile hectic beautiful-faced, half-idiot-looking boy'.[17] In burlesque, light opera and Pantomime, women also played men's roles with considerable gusto. But there was a Victorian nervousness about this tradition: in a speech in 1906, W. S. Gilbert related that when he and Sullivan had formed their partnership in 1875 they had laid down various ground rules, one of which was that 'on artistic principles, no man should play a woman's part and no woman a man's'.[18] They also agreed that no actress in their plays 'should be required to wear a dress that she could not wear with absolute propriety at a private fancy ball'. His 'artistic principles' seem to have been based firmly on his moral ones, and he guarded the reputations of his female Savoyards so fiercely that in the 1880s his theatre was nicknamed 'The Savoy Boarding School'. None of these actresses however, nor the Pantomime Principal Boys, nor even many of the Music Hall comediennes who sang occasional songs in cross-dress, were really 'impersonators'; but they did create a strong tradition which made possible the more thoroughgoing impersonations which became increasingly popular from the late 1880s. While most of these performers were judged as little more 'than giggling girls in trousers', using their male clothes to exhibit their female characteristics, there was nevertheless a developing genre into which Vesta Tilley was able to move. The extreme sophistication and range of her impersonations shifted the whole genre in a new direction. Her immediate successors, Hetty King and Ella Shields, both − rather resentfully − acknowledged their debt to her, and later Marlene Dietrich was explicit in asserting that Vesta Tilley had made possible the whole new mode of gender impersonation for women; a tradition subsequently developed by Greta Garbo in film, Beatrice Lillie in revue, and most recently by Annie Lennox in popular music.

Still there were rigorous limits to what Vesta Tilley felt able to do with her act. She never played unattractive men; even her rakes 'got drunk with elegance'. As mentioned earlier, the only fully serious dramatic role she ever played was a sketch of 'The Death of Chatterton'; but as the poet she presented was only seventeen at the time of his suicide this fitted more easily into the 'pathetic youth' tradition than might at first appear. She did not play violent men, old men or villainous men: nobody did, despite the fact that female-impersonators, of whom there were a far greater number, were developing in all areas of the theatre more and more savage or slapstick representations of women as old, greedy, ugly, ludicrous or violent.

There was of course a social advantage for male-impersonators once performance drag had been confined to the stage. It was infinitely safer because the artist could, if she chose, create a secondary persona — a so-called 'private life' — of absolute respectability, or at least of conformity to what was socially regarded as 'feminine'. Subsequent male-impersonators, or 'gender-benders' have learned this device: both Dietrich and more recently Annie Lennox have given interviews in which they firmly disassociate their 'real' self from the images they present in their 'public' persona. They require that we do not question what gender they 'really are', but only that we admire their skills of dissimulation. They have not used this new space and safety to create a radical assault on the state of 'maleness' nor to advance a more serious, social critique of men's behaviour. It is as though, like Vesta Tilley, they are still anxious to have the audience know that offstage they are different, they are 'really' perfectly safe, and present no danger to the superior sex.

In her book *Mother Camp*, a sociological study of contemporary *female*-impersonators in the USA, Esther Newton draws a distinction between two groups of impersonators. (She stresses that in their 'private lives' both groups are homosexual, and that both groups have evolved their strategies as ways of dealing with their stigmatization, so they are therefore not a perfect parallel with male-impersonators):

There are two different patterns of being a female impersonator. Each pattern consists of a characteristic presentation of self, lifestyle, and attitudes towards basic life problems. I will distinguish the patterns by the terms 'street' impersonators and 'stage' impersonators . . . the street pattern is a *fusion* of the 'street fairy' life with the profession of female impersonation . . . Street impersonators are never off-stage. As one stage impersonator told me, all they have to do to go to work is put on a wig . . . The stage pattern on the other hand *segregates* the stigma from the personal life by limiting it to the stage context as much as possible. The work is viewed as a profession with goals and standards, rather than as a job. Stage impersonators are individualistic, relatively 'respectable' . . . Stage impersonators contrast most strikingly with street impersonators in their public presentation of themselves . . . (They) *all* insisted on two points; first, that off-stage they restrict their contacts with other impersonators and second, that in public places they attempt to pass as 'normal' or at least appear as inconspicuous as possible . . . they act on basically middle-class conceptions of appropriate living arrangements . . . Stage impersonators are concerned with 'professionalism' and can be articulate about the history of impersonation (most know about drag in the old vaudeville days) goals and standards of performance . . . They stress whatever personal contact they have had with [legitimate show-business] 'stars'. At the same time they express nothing but contempt for queens who refuse to segregate their activities into clearly defined work and private domains.[19]

The point here is that *all* successful male-impersonators fall into the category of 'stage' impersonators: Esther Newton adds that 'The street life is by definition anti-establishment', but there is no 'street life' of this sort for women who are impersonators, there has never been such a community. For male-impersonators to survive, they have to find a supportive community of *men*; they cannot hold those men up to the same sort of ridicule that it is possible for men to hold women up to because they are dependent on them. Often this dependence is economic or emotional; always it is based on the fact that male values and cultural determinants are dominant. Men have the capacity to control almost all of the channels through which male-impersonators might seek their necessary audience – both in the crude sense of owning the theatres, the press and the media; and in the cultural sense of creating and manipulating the images and perceptions of 'femininity'.

The best a male-impersonator can do for herself is to seek a status of gender-indeterminancy; and, alas, that does not really exist. In this sense all her followers learned a lesson from Joan of Arc – the only home of the androgyne is in heaven, and if necessary men will help to speed her way there as swiftly as possible. If martyrdom is not what you are seeking, it is vital that male-impersonation is underlined by a twofold admission: one, that you are different from other women because you *understand* men — so that they can allow you to be 'one of the boys'; and two, at the same time, you are a 'real woman', prepared to demonstrate true 'womanliness' whenever you are required to do so.

I am trying to suggest that while there is a potential sexual radicalism in women assuming male dress, it has not worked to the actual advancement of women. Although, since Vesta Tilley's retirement in 1920, the gender distinction presented through clothing has become more complex this route to exploring female power has remained a dead end. Diana Simmonds, a feminist journalist and critic, commented when we discussed this problem:

Actually I can't see Vesta Tilley even being able to get up on stage in 1985. Because although it is acceptable, indeed virtually *de rigueur*, for women to adopt aspects of male dress, it has become somehow unacceptable for women to *adopt male attire* even in entertainment. There is a huge difference (about as wide as the Grand Canyon) between the two: aspects of male dress on the one hand, and male dress on the other. It is an accepted part of fashion now for women to adopt apparent ambiguity, so a female cross-dressing entertainer would have to go a very long way into adopting a male persona before she would be much different from her audience. The extent of that journey would I think, render her even less acceptable in polite society than Vesta Tilley was to hers. For a female performer to get a cross-dressing act together today would be really radical — assuming that she didn't hark back to Marlene or take the easy way out with Annie Hall or merely tease like Annie Lennox.[20]

She would have to create and expose real confusion. She would also have to create an audience willing to explore that confusion, not vicariously in terms of plot, but reflectively in terms of their own gender identity. She would have to make clear within the terms of her act that all gender roles are 'impersonations', acts, performances, in as much as gender roles are socially constructed, and she would have to do this without consenting to the myth of male superiority, that is without denying biological and social 'womanliness':

The reader may now ask how I define womanliness or where I draw the line between genuine womanliness and the 'masquerade'. My suggestion is not, however, that there is any such difference; whether radical or superficial, they are the same thing.[21]

The proof of this statement lies in the very different forms of male and female drag.

At the same time that Vesta Tilley was dressing up as a soldier and singing challenging lines like, 'Girls if you want to love a soldier, you can all love ME', Constance Lytton was dying for her 'militancy' as a suffragette, women from the middle-class suffrage movement and the working-class trade union movement were 'declaring war' on an unjust government which deprived women and the working class of their basic rights. It is worth asking which group did most to challenge gender role assumptions about the Angel in the Home. This should not, however, be seen as a straightforward moralistic judgement of Vesta Tilley, who never made any such claims for herself. (Indeed after her retirement, suddenly forgetting that she had been one of the best-paid and most publicly known figures of the pre-war decade, she would make announcements about the unsuitability of women for public life.) It is more a question about a strategy for now. For, despite all the changes in the social function of women since the last century — helped in part by both Vesta Tilley and the industrial and political militants — there has been no real change either in the conviction that gender is a fixed, immutable, innate, 'natural' reality, nor in the underlying belief that men are superior to women.

FINALE

What is abnormal in Life stands in normal relations to Art. It is
the only thing in Life which stands in normal relations to Art.
  Oscar Wilde [1]

So what was it that she did? There was something extraordinary in her act; it transcended class and national
boundaries. She showed her legs and sang songs whose sexual
content now seems almost blindingly unsubtle, and yet the
arch-puritan of the Music Halls, Sir Oswald Stoll, not only
loved her and was her friend, but also wrote:

To Vesta Tilley art has been nature all her life. That is why the
nature of her art saw no need to descend to the baser natural levels
. . . The power to attract the largest following, and to give the most
profitable advertisement to the stage, has always been in the hands of
artistes who never descend to the *double entendre* of the smoking
room as the staple of their work . . . The public went to hear Vesta
Tilley because her work could be done by her alone.[2]

It is almost impossible now to understand or even imagine
what she did with an audience. Every time one has been on a
bus and wondered even for a few seconds which sex the
person opposite with jeans and longish hair was distances us
too far from the 1900s to understand. There are other
problems too. Vesta Tilley did make recordings, and on them
– reissued now as part of the sentimentality for 'the good
old days' – you can hear a pure voice, not strong, but of

extraordinary clarity. But then all Music Hall performers held large and rowdy audiences without any form of amplification: clarity and projection are common to them all. The songs seem mildly amusing, if not particularly exciting. But the crudity of early recording worked very much against Music Hall style: the singer had to stand with her mouth pressed against the recording machine, and the technical limitations prevented almost all movement.

A male-impersonator's act is absolutely dependent on its visual impact. It is wrong to think of Vesta Tilley, or indeed most of the Music Hall greats, primarily as singers. Although the song was the vehicle of their acts, for most of them it was not the true centre. Throughout the golden era of Music Hall there were no 'stand-up comedians' as we now know them; but spoken comedy and visual 'business' were integral to the presentation of the song. From the earliest days, singers like Sam Cowell (1840–64) were creating their effect by giving a humorous commentary on their own tragic ballads in an elaborate burlesque of the sententious and pompous style adopted by the Chairmen, and indeed by too many Victorian 'worthies'. Sam Cowell would precede a verse about the wronged heroine's tragic suicide, with a phrase like,

Now this is the most melancholy part of it and shows what the progeny was druv to in conskivance of the mangled obstropolousness and ferocity of the inconsiderable parient.[3]

The modern presentation of many Music Hall songs has been adversely affected by this factor: many of the songs simply cannot be written down without the patter. The best recorders of Music Hall songs, like P. Davison in his collection *The Songs of British Music Hall*, sensibly include a transcription of the patter. Bessie Bellwood's 'What Cheer, Ria', for instance, needs its patter not only in order to make any narrative sense of the music, but also to integrate the verses and the chorus. By the end of his highly influential life, Dan Leno had developed an act which was much more nearly that of a 'stand-up comic' than it was to the song-and-dance tradition. The experience of Pantomime acting, where performers maintained a character and forwarded a narrative in between their musical numbers, affected Music Hall technique in important ways.

This mixture of song and 'business' was the mark of Music Hall: by the 1900s there were far more comediennes and serio-comediennes than there were straight singers. The increasing number of variety acts − magicians, animal acts and stunts − may even be explained by the need to vary the comic element with something more emotionally arresting. This type of act was absorbed in the 1920s into revue, but perhaps the best modern parallel would be the black women 'rappers' like Millie Jackson, Laura Lee and Shirley Brown. As an additional problem for Music Hall historians the patter was more often ad-libbed than scripted − improvised out of the nightly relationship between performer and audience.

This intimacy and consent between audience and performer, unusual in that it continued even when the Halls had become huge and the audiences numbered thousands, makes it well nigh impossible to reconstruct the old acts: the performers' material may be available, but the audiences are not. Davison describes the relationship:

In Music Hall the aim of breaking continuity is simple − to raise a laugh − but the effect is more complex. Involvement with the *act* is broken . . . a relationship is developed between the person of the performer and the audience, rather than with his persona. But the detachment from the persona (the breaking of empathy) is not at the expense of overall involvement; for the audience though momentarily detached and alienated thereafter becomes more deeply involved.[4]

An involvement to which they, in normal social life singularly powerless and oppressed, have not only consented to, but have themselves implemented.

The great stars of Music Hall were those who could create and sustain this new, responsive involvement; it was what the audience − never a passive and often a savage one − demanded of them; it called for something more than just extreme skill in performance — it demanded a particularly strong stage presence, a personality.

Vesta Tilley's version of this 'alienation and new involvement' was different from most: she was always a tightly-rehearsed and non-spontaneous performer who never engaged in much direct repartee with her audience, or even used her speaking voice. This must have been partly because she took herself extremely seriously (despite her 'comic' act) and was not interested in self-parody. But more importantly, because of the very nature of her act, and particularly because she never sang 'false bass' but always her own treble, the vital 'breaking of continuity' — the gap between her persona and her person — had already occurred; as a gender impersonator that gap was integral to her act; it occurred constantly in her very appearance. It was inevitably, unnervingly present.

And in this sense Vesta Tilley's act necessarily depended on her presence on the stage even more than other performers, and her absence makes it even harder to understand, from our contemporary perspective, the exact nature of her grip over an audience. Her impersonation did not lie in her voice (which was female) but in her mime and presentation — or rather in the conflict between the two. The only medium that could have given her immortality was film and this may explain her willingness to work for so long, and for free, with W. G. Gibbons on the synchronization of film-track and sound-track, while she found the making of a silent film unutterably boring and distasteful. 'She is not so much a singer as a comic mime who chooses to accompany her act with her own voice.'[5]

Another element, much commented on by those who saw her, but completely lost in the available recordings, was her (not unique) counter-timing: distorting the 'natural' musical rhythm of her songs by dragging out or speeding up different passages for dramatic effect. It says, in fact, a great deal about the skill of Music Hall orchestras that they were able to accompany performers at all, since they had new numbers to learn almost weekly and the rehearsal times were notoriously inadequate. Once, in America, Vesta Tilley was to perform

with a 'straight' theatre orchestra, and despite lengthy
rehearsals the musicians were so incapable of following her that
Walter de Frece had to take over from the professional
conductor and — since he did not know how to conduct — hum
at them in a low tone through her pauses and distortions of the
rhythm.

Since the timing, the impersonation, the 'business' and the
relationship with the audience are all lost in these early
cylinder and wax-cut recordings, to get any impression of her
act at all we have to rely on contemporary accounts. Even
here there seems a certain sense of bafflement:

What was her great attraction? That it was great is, I think,
undisputed. She could fill any hall anywhere. Women liked her and
to say that is to say much, for women were not then fond of Music
Hall artistes. Of all the English artistes to go to America she was
certainly our greatest success. She had personality, but so had all the
great Music Hall performers . . . in addition she had distinction and
grace and daintiness and very great charm. Her small figure,
exquisitely tailored, caught and held attention . . . her attractive and
intelligent face lit by beautiful and humorous eyes, had a rare look of
benignity . . . the small but shapely head was beautifully poised on
as trim a figure as most people had ever seen . . . I think it must
have been the delicacy of her work more than anything else that
made Vesta Tilley popular . . . she never strained or shouted, there
was no coarseness of any kind in her performance . . . she was as
delicate and fastidious as a racehorse. The crowd loved her and the
crowd was right.[6]

Other critics come up with wonderful simplicities which are
hardly illuminating for us:

She displayed immaculate dress clothes with an ease and elegance no
mere man ever aims to. Her success was due to the fact that every
male hopes one day he may wear a dress suit thus, instead of have it
'hang all over him'.[7]

Obviously there was something very knowing and psychologically profound in her act: Willson Disher, quoted earlier, said that she exposed men to themselves — forced them to see themselves anew; W. R. Titterton almost wryly acknowledged how well she understood men's 'foibles'. But underlying this dangerous knowledge, she projected a powerful message of innocence. Alfred Butt, who wrote her entry in the *Dictionary of National Biography* and knew her well, found her

unique, a frail simple little thing, just radiating the joy of life . . . as light and graceful as a child . . . it was a sheer joy to see and hear her portray one of her songs . . . a sincere expression of all the simple emotions of life.[8]

This innocence seems to have captivated even her most censorious commentators. Titterton, a sentimental moralist, says she had 'the soul of a naive child' and that 'she charmed me with her freshness . . . her unspoiled rollicking boyishness'.[9] Stoll, an obsessive puritan, claims that she 'never descended to the *doubles entendres* of the smoking room'. But if you look at her material, bearing in mind she was that sensitive thing — a woman dressed as a man — it is hard not to wonder what they *would* have called a *double entendre*, what they would have thought of as vulgar, what kind of naive children they were acquainted with. 'Following in Father's Footsteps' was one of Vesta Tilley's most successful numbers: by popular request she sung it at her farewell performance at the Coliseum. It was written for her by E. W. Rogers, in 1902. Rogers wrote a number of her other hit songs, like 'When a Fellah Has Turned Sixteen', 'The Midnight Son' and 'It's Part of a P'liceman's Duty' and he was one of the writers most sensitive to the sort of material that was making Vesta Tilley so pre-eminent in the 1890s and 1900s. For 'Following in Father's Footsteps', Vesta Tilley wore an Eton suit and cap (shades of Mary Pickford in 'Poor Little Rich Girl' in 1917). The tone of the song is typical of many of her numbers and is worth looking at:

To follow in your father's footsteps is a motto for each
  boy,
And following in Father's footsteps is a thing I much
  enjoy.
My mother caught me out one evening, up the West End
  on the spree,
She said, 'Where are you going?', but I answered, 'Don't
  ask *me*!'

Chorus
I'm following in Father's footsteps, I'm following dear old
  dad.
He's just in front with a big fine gal, so I thought I'd have
  one as well.
I don't know where he's going, but when he gets there I'll
  be glad!
I'm following in Father's footsteps, yes, I'm following the
  dear old dad.

Pa said that to the North of England he on bus'ness had to
  go,
To Charing Cross he went, and there he booked, I booked
  first class as well,
I found myself that night in Paris; to the clergyman next
  door
I answered, when he asked, 'What are you in this gay place
  for?'

Chorus
I'm following in Father's footsteps, I'm following dear old
  dad;
He's trav'ling now for his firm you see, in fancy goods it
  seems to me.
I don't know where he's going, but when he gets there I'll
  be glad,
I'm following in Father's footsteps, just following the dear
  old dad.

At Margate with papa I toddled out to have a good old
  swim,
I didn't know the proper place to bathe, so I left it all to
  him.
I found myself among some ladies, and enjoyed it; so did
  pa!
Till ma yelled, 'Percy, fie for shame.' Said I, 'It's alright
  ma!'

Chorus

I'm following in Father's footsteps, I'm following the dear
  old dad,
He's just out there with fair Miss Jupp to show me how to
  hold girls up.
I'm going to hold her next, ma, but when he drops her I'll
  be glad;
I'm following in Father's footsteps, I'm following the dear
  old dad.

To dinner up in town last night I went, and pa went there
  as well,
How many 'lemonades' we had – my word! I really
  couldn't tell.
At two a.m. pa started off for home like *this*, so did I,
Folks said, 'Mind where you're going' but I simply made
  reply,

Chorus

'I'm following in Father's footsteps, I'm following dear old
  dad,
He's wobbling on in front you see, and 'pon my word he's
  worse than me.'
My mother caught me out one evening, up the West End
  on the spree,
She said, 'Where are you going?', and I answered, 'Don't
  ask me!
I'm following in Father's footsteps, I'm following dear old
  dad.'[10]

Now I'm not trying to suggest that this is a particularly lewd song, and whether it comes across as innocent or 'knowing' must obviously depend on its performance; but Oswald Stoll, who remember, would not let Ida Farren be carried off *his* stage rolled in a carpet, on the grounds that it was morally suspect, found this number 'untouched by the *double entendre* of the smoking room'.

Of course 'Father' was one of the stock butts of Music Hall comedy; along with 'swells' and people who tried to be 'posh'. It would be impossible to give a list of the songs that ridiculed him — by men (like George Robey) as often as by women. Nothing makes clearer the extraordinary power of the Victorian patriarch of all classes over the lives of his family than the constancy with which he is deflated, duped, caught out and ridiculed — by wives, children, lodgers and friends — in the safe space of Music Hall comedy. But this explanation of the song's acceptability does not cover the insinuations in other songs, like 'Obliging Brother Bertie', about another, only slightly older, young man who has a very shy older brother, whom he 'obliges' by courting his girlfriend, attending his parties and so on. One verse of the song goes:

My brother Bertie's a bit run down
So ma said to him one day
'You must go and see the doctor dear', but he
Just funked it in the usual way.
Ma said, 'Harold, you'll have to go instead',
But I quickly answered 'no'.
Till Papa told me, that the doctor I'd to see,
Was a Lady, then I said, 'Rightho.'

I'm obligin' brother Bertie,
I'm doing it for dear old Bert.
Now ev'ry day I'm there you bet
Bertie won't be better for a long time yet
I'm obliging brother Bertie, all the details I won't tell,
But I've learned a thing or two for Bertie
And a trifle for myself as well.[11]

Apart from the gratuitous insult from one woman profes- sional to another, it is well-nigh impossible to see how anyone can not have read suggestiveness into these lyrics. In fact the obliging youth gets sent down by the magistrate for being drunk and disorderly; and when he's told that the boy was only 'obliging brother Bertie' pronounces, 'Well you'd better take a month inside for Bertie, and a couple for yourself as well.' So that in performance this youth was the butt of the joke, rather than the admired and cocky hero of the tale; but the 'purity' of the lyrics is scarcely affected by this.

Of course these were by no means the only type of song that Vesta Tilley presented: one of the reasons given for her success was the size and range of her repertoire. Just as she had started as a child with a sentimental drawing-room ballad, 'Come into the Garden Maud', so she continued to render these. 'After the Ball', which made its composer the American Charles K. Harris into a millionaire, was the first song to have sheet music sales of over five million, and was one of Vesta Tilley's most successful sentimental songs. (It was also one of the few songs that she did not have exclusive rights to, and it was sung with almost equal success by Charles Godfrey, which indicates that there was nothing in this type of number which required cross-dressing for its effect.) It is an interest- ing song for Vesta Tilley to have chosen because it opens with an appeal from a 'little maid' for her uncle to tell her a story − the breaking of his girlfriend's heart 'years, years ago' is apparently triggered by this request. 'Sweetheart May' and 'Mary and John', which were both written for her, and 'The Girls I Left Behind Me', which was not, were all songs of this type: sentimental ballads with highly singable tunes, popular beyond the Halls and completely inoffensive.

Now, of course, Vesta Tilley is remembered more for her 'masher' or dandy songs than for the others. There was 'Burlington Bertie − the Boy with the Hyde Park Drawl', (not to be confused with Ella Shield's satirical alternative, 'Burlington Bertie from Bow', in which the apparently dash- ing young swell turns out to be a fake, an impoverished, broken-down rake). Vesta Tilley's Bertie was also not what he appeared, but to his credit: he seemed to be nothing but an effete upper-class layabout, yet

> What price Burlington Bertie,
> The boy with the Hyde Park drawl?
> What price Burlington Bertie
> The boy with the Bond Street crawl?
> He'll fight and he'll die like an Englishman
> Forgive all his folly we can.
> Says old John Bull: 'I plainly see
> These Burlington Boys are the boys for me.'[12]

'Algy – the Piccadilly Johnnie with the Little Glass Eye' has already been discussed in reference to its amazing success in America, where Vesta Tilley commissioned and toured a whole play based on the character. She bought the rights for the song on the off-chance from its composer, H. B. Norris, for £5, 'even though I thought that masher songs had been rather played out', and first sang it in Oxford at the end of the 1880s. One of the reasons for its success was that one chorus, always a different one, instead of being sung was 'laughed through', a high, inane laugh in time to the music, which endeared itself enormously to the audience. She also had a 'Monty from Monte Carlo', a gambler so successful that, when performing the song, Vesta Tilley used to shower the stage with gold coins which she released from sleeves, pockets and even a specially prepared hollow cane. This genre of song was not invented by Vesta Tilley, but was enormously popular. Starting with George Leybourne's 'Champagne Charlie' in 1866, there followed a great string of alliterative dandies; contemporaneous with Vesta Tilley, Tom Leamore was singing these songs, including 'Percy from Pimlico', with considerable success.

She also had a series of songs which were specifically directed towards her skill for detailed presentation of professional types drawn from across the whole social spectrum: soldiers, sailors, policemen, messenger-boys and curates.

What they offered was a chance for Vesta Tilley to demonstrate the accuracy of her observations and to dress up: they
all belonged, as Willson Disher remarks,

to that side of masculinity which is clothes conscious. All the young
men she pretended to be are proud of what they wear — all of them,
from the one in 'Etons' to the one in khaki.[13]

Yet another set of songs, her least attractive to my mind,
although they were also successful, criticize women, 'the
girls'. I think they are 'giving too much away', and again
emphasize the identification of Vesta Tilley's stage persona
with maleness. In 1898 she introduced 'Angels Without
Wings' by G. Ware, which caused a sensation by being in
waltz time and which had the following chorus:

Angels, angels, angels without wings,
Simple, very simple, very pious little things,
Angels, angels floating about,
Like the men you're angels when you're not found out.[14]

'For the Sake of the Dear Little Girls' was another similar
song:

Oh, the girls are the ruin of man,
Since the days of Eve and Adam.
Nice little things, want little rings,
Want little diamonds and pearls.
Oh, the girls are the ruin of man,
To change a Miss into a Madam,
Isn't it funny, we spend all our money
Just for the sake of the girls.[15]

Finally, there were the military/patriotic songs. Long before
1914 she was presenting characters from the services, and
particularly from the army. The general line of Music Hall
songs, for various reasons, preferred sailors to soldiers, but
although Vesta Tilley did the occasional midshipman number,
accompanied by hornpipe dancing, it was her widely varying
soldiers who made her famous. The immensely popular 'Jolly

Good Luck to the Girl who Loves a Soldier' was written for her by K. Lyle in 1905 — long before the wave of militaristic fervour had swept the nation. Titterton describes her presentation of this number with obvious delight:

Out steps a Tommy from the wings in Brodrick cap and crimson cloth, striding jauntily with the chest out and a slapping cane. This is irresistible; these quick-step movements seize us; this merry saucy face with its sideways jerk sets our blood dancing. With what delicious jerky precision the feet tap heel and toe! How the whole body keeps time within itself as if it were a battalion. This Tommy is so virile, so vain, so self-possessed, so jolly — you long to be up and after him . . . here is the very type of Tommy — joyous, impudent and imperturbable. What jealous loving observation went into the making of this figure! What wondrous stroke of the wizard's wand it was gave life to this clay! The first verse finishes, the singer makes her dominant pause on the first syllable of the chorus, and then romps away with it:

Here's — jolly good luck to the girl who loves a soldier.
  Girls — have you been there?
You know that military men
  Always do their duty everywhere.
Jolly good luck to the girl who loves a soldier!
  All good boys are we.
Girls! If you'd like to love a soldier,
  You can all — love — me.

With a tantarara and a tantareon the cane makes desperate rhythmic lunges, circles, circles, is sheathed dexterously in the left hand, and Tommy is at attention, stiff and wooden to the neck, and beaming above it with a beautiful, broad seraphic smile.[16]

The bumptious and swaggering Tommy, even before he became the tragic hero of the trenches, represented a working-class version of the upper-class masher, and her technique used in performing both of these types is not dissimilar. It is worth noting that the 1890s and 1900s was the period of the English *fin de siècle* and while the artists of the

'Decadence' might not seem, especially to themselves, to have had much in common with the artistes of the Halls, Baudelaire, their hero, had written in *Le Peintre de la Vie Moderne* that the only heroes suitable to the times were the Soldier and the Dandy. He also considered that 'the good and the beautiful are of their nature artificial'. It is interesting then that Vesta Tilley represented both figures with perfect and necessary artificiality.

But it was of course the war that brought her military types into full focus and made her a heroine to the troops. These songs are not unsophisticated, and though they are finally adulatory, they are also ironic and unsentimental. 'Six Days Leave' is about a soldier returning from the front, exhausted by the demands of his family:

It's a fine time for a soldier
When he's home on six days leave,
Must see Aunt Maria, must see Uncle Jim,
Tell them what the general said,
And what I said to him.
It's a fine time for a soldier
But with all due respect and regard
Next time they give me six days leave
Let them give me six months 'hard'.[17]

Another number, 'A Bit of a Blighty One', celebrated, quite tenderly, the wounded Tommy. She sang this often on the Halls and on her innumerable tours around hospitals: 'It was because of her delicate burlesque that the rather hideous hospital blue, the red tie and khaki cap became a fit habit for heroes.'[18] However, the song that earned her the nickname of 'England's Best Recruiting Sergeant', and which was taken up by the War Office as the basis of a recruiting poster, was 'The Army of Today's All Right' in which a very new, very cocky, very proud recruit offers comfort to those at home, reassuring them:

It's all right, it's all right now
There's no need to worry anymore.
Who said the army wasn't strong,
They soon found out that they were wrong
When Kitchener came along.
So let the band play and shout 'hooray'
I'll show the Germans how to fight,
I joined the army yesterday
So the army of today's all right.[19]

Oddly enough, the songs that made her unique among the 'buxom swells', which changed the course of popular cross-dressing and which created the atmosphere for the 1920s revue and cabaret male-impersonators, are almost entirely forgotten now. Increasingly, in the years after 1890, Vesta Tilley introduced a series of songs which looked at the pretensions not of the working class but of the new middle class. Songs mocking social pretensions had been common in Music Hall from the start. But Vesta Tilley located a new audience, the suburban lower-middle classes, the clerks and shopkeepers, the skilled industrial artisans and overseers, who also had their social pretensions; a stream of songs pinned them down, not unkindly but accurately. There is 'The Seaside Sultan':

He's the seaside sultan, he's the monarch of the pier,
Of the beach he's the Shah,
Of the promenade the Czar,
All the ladies in his company will lurk.
It's an awful blow
When he has to go — back to work.[20]

'Sydney's Holiday', 'When a Fellah Has Turned Sixteen' and 'The Afternoon Parade' are all songs about young men who pretend to a social status to which, according to the social code of their times they are not 'entitled'. And yet for all their foolishness, Vesta Tilley appears to be unable to condemn them: she was after all one of them herself, someone using 'appearance', dress, 'style', to move upwards socially.

It was these songs that gave a new depth to her work after her marriage and gained her her special standing among male-impersonators. When Titterton first saw her perform he thought

she harped too much on that old frayed string of getting drunk in evening dress and flirting with unchaperoned young women. Doubtless flirting is an eternal topic, but not necessarily flirting in a disguise of swallow-tails and swallowed liquor, on just one acre of London, at just one time of day. It seemed too much a tribute to the lords of wealth and station. I liked the Cockney courtships of Chevalier better.

But Vesta Tilley has gone far since then. She began by imitating individual eccentricities; now she creates and characterizes types. Then her territory stretched from Piccadilly to the Charing Cross Road; now she has annexed Aldershot, the seaside and the quarterdeck; all types of fledgling manhood (I speak in a Pickwickian and artistic sense) are her lawful prey.[21]

These songs were unique to Vesta Tilley. They were an entirely new genre, which she created to meet the aspirations of the new audience of 'respectable' Music Hall. They were also songs about the class from which her husband came; both of them identified this audience very accurately and incorporated it into popular entertainment – Walter de Frece in the Music Hall theatres and shows that he offered, and Vesta Tilley in her own material. Her success was followed by others, but by making the life-styles of the petty bourgeoisie a central concern of her art, she foreshadowed the great changes that the cinema was to make to popular culture after the war.

Had it not been for the war it seems likely that Vesta Tilley would have done fewer military songs, just as she was doing fewer dandy songs, concentrating instead on songs of social satire against young men with pretensions, and against 'the girls' themselves. However, after 1914 the young men whom she had exposed became the heroes against whom no word could be uttered: like so much of the Edwardian period, Vesta Tilley's songs can only be seen through the filter of the wasteful, painful and lethal war. Willson Disher, one of the most sensitive of the Music Hall commentators, shows in his own writing how the war experience changed and senti-mentalized public perception.

'By the Sad Sea Waves' illustrated her process. She picked on a poor little London 'chappie' earning fifteen shillings a week and spending every penny he could spare on haberdashery for a week at Brighton, where he hoped to pass muster on the promenade as a real masher. The story goes against the hero . . . back at business, he found the beauty he met at Brighton was the girl in the cook-shop. No doubt the song-writer had a little mockery in mind. In performance, however, this was magically translated. What we felt when Vesta Tilley showed him to us was not derision but pathos. She felt for him and with him and her tenderness over that little scrap of humanity was evident in all the portraits she painted from that time onwards.

Crotchety veterans might wonder what on earth the younger generation was coming to . . . but Vesta Tilley knew . . . We recognised the weedy youth in khaki; we had seen him in 'By the Sad Sea Waves'. Unknown to the crotchety veterans in club armchairs, there had always been in him the stuff heroes are made of. He was to win the battles they would do their damndest to lose. He would man their trenches as cheerfully as he had once lined seaside esplanades: and the only one to have prophetically recognised it in the past was not himself — for he died without gaining consciousness that he was a hero — but Vesta Tilley.

Looking back on the junior clerk, we can see how she had discerned pluck even in his drudgery to buy haberdashery . . . When the time came to answer those cartoons of him as a tailor's dummy with a novelette, she signalised his vindication with 'I joined the army yesterday, so the Army of today's all right.' On the surface it was a joke — but only on the surface.[22]

It is important to remember that Vesta Tilley worked her 'magical translation' not simply by looking at her husband refusing to touch cash without gloves on, and loving him for his determination to fight his way out of the class trap, and then finding nice ironic songs to sing. At the base of her success lay an extraordinary talent for detailed observation and an 'infinite capacity for taking pains'. There are innumerable Vesta Tilley anecdotes which illustrate this almost obsessive attention to detail: when she sang 'Six Days Leave' she spent literally hours at railway stations watching the troops disembarking, and then insisted that her own knapsack be filled to the regulation weight, as the straw-stuffed one with which she had originally rehearsed did not swing correctly. She was frequently praised in the press for the astonishing accuracy of her gestures and particularly for her miming and 'business' — 'the perfect mistress of the art of walking';[23] for the extraordinary speed with which she could shift from one mood to another (the drunken lurch suddenly obtruded into the boyish gait in 'Following Father's Footsteps', for instance) and for the careful distinctions that she made between classes and occupations. It was this remarkable attention to detail above all that separated her from the mass of male-impersonators — those 'giggling girls thinly disguised' whose popularity waned through the 1890s as she demonstrated more and more clearly what could be done with the genre.

And beneath these details the general attention to perfection went on. Although she was always extremely slight, she was still prepared to spend over an hour before every night's performance, padding and constructing her figure so that the precise degree of Titterton's 'female curves' was perfectly controlled. She worked under the additional disadvantage of having to wear many close-fitting costumes and she also always wore men's underclothes during performances.[24] Women's underclothes of her time were hardly functional in terms of performance: gender divisions were marked right down to the skin in Victorian and Edwardian England. It is interesting, however, that Esther Newton found in the male drag community a very strong disapproval of wearing 'female underclothes': 'female impersonation', said one of her respondents, 'is so involved with the transvestite thing that we all fear . . . the typical transy [transvestite] thing is to wear feminine attire *underneath* . . . the drag queen hardly ever does this.'[25] Transvestism means for this community wearing some item of feminine apparel, like frilly panties, which is 'not related to the necessities of the performance'. Obviously it would be silly to draw too close a parallel between the ethos of female-impersonators in America in the 1960s and male-impersonators in London in the 1890s and 1900s, but there is often a quality of almost exhibitionist obsession about the way in which Vesta Tilley spoke and wrote about her costuming and her attention to detail. She herself, in her *Recollections* and in an article for the *Pelican Christmas Annual* (1906–7), 'The Tale of a Wig', goes into enormous detail in relating how her wig was constructed. She refused to cut off her hair, which remained long and curly throughout her life, but she also sought a perfect silhouette in performance. She had to spend hours plaiting her own hair into tiny braids and coiling them around her head – in a style not dissimilar to corn-rows. In private life she won a number of bets, she claimed, with people so convinced by the authenticity of her short hair that they assumed her more womanly tresses were the wig.

All observers, even those who were not her fans, acknow-ledge that Vesta Tilley's performance was of an exceptionally high standard. After her father's death she took direct control over the content of her own act. She chose her own songs and, together with her tailor, Samuelson Son & Linney, an eminent men's outfitter of Maddox Street, (off Bond Street), created her costumes completely – she even changed socks for every character. She projected this immaculate and precise image on the stage in performances that were always impeccably timed, researched, rehearsed and presented. She was both talented and diligent.

But as has already been discussed, success on the Halls depended not just on the performance in isolation, but on the performer's relationship with the audience. So it is necessary to look at her audience and at what they found in her act which so endeared her to them. Part of the reason for her success with her male audience has already been suggested: she offered them intelligently and humorously a flattering mirror of themselves, which, since she was a woman, they did not find threatening. But it is important to remember that the majority of her fans were women; what was it that they found so attractive in her performance? What did her male-impersonation mean to them?

It is now hard to tell. There were no women journalists covering Music Hall; few educated, serious middle-class women would even admit to attending Music Hall. The nineteenth-century feminists had deliberately turned their backs on questions of sexuality and gender representation, as well as on the 'frivolity' (left-wing women) and the 'vulgarity' (bourgeois feminists) of the Halls. The only woman I have spoken to who can remember Vesta Tilley performing before the war could hum snatches of her songs and describe her costumes, but could only say, 'My God she was funny, so funny; you cannot imagine how funny she was. And of course she was a lady, not like some of them.'[26] (This commentator was not referring to Walter de Frece's knighthood, but to some quality in Vesta Tilley herself.) None the less it remains a fact that although the people who wrote about her were men, they all acknowledged that her real fans were women, and usually married working-class women who named their children after her, travelled round the country to see her perform and bought her postcards in their thousands.

I have come to believe that this enthusiasm for her work grew out of the radical changes that took place in women's life-styles and expectations at the end of the nineteenth century, and which were reflected in Music Hall as the principal popular entertainment of its day. It is usually claimed that British Music Hall, like American Vaudeville, but unlike the Berlin *Kabaretten* or the French *Café-concerts*, failed to engage politically; and that such politics as it did espouse were crudely conservative, imperialist and jingoistic. This is something of a simplification: it is true of course that the very word 'jingoism' was introduced into popular speech by the enormous success of G. H. McDermott's Crimean War song, 'We Don't Want to Fight, But By Jingo if We Do', but it is too easily forgotten that, successful though this was, Herbert Campbell — later óne of the major comedians of Pantomime and the Halls — originally made his name singing an extremely popular satire of this song with a chorus that went, 'I don't want to fight, I'll be slaughtered if I do . . . I'd *let* the Russians have Constantinople.' There were other successful songs, even less patriotic in their sentiments, including one that discussed birth control and the royal family, which has the Queen, worried about the number of her children, concluding, 'So Albert, dear Albert we'll do it no more.' Sam Torr and Harry Rickards, among others, sang songs in the late 1880s criticizing the Queen in savage terms: Torr's chorus concluded, 'But oh my, shan't I be glad when the Prince of Wales is King.'[27]

By and large, though, when it came to party politics the Music Hall successes were mainly cynical or resigned. This detachment must primarily have stemmed from a sense of powerlessness — much of the audience of the Halls was not even enfranchized until 1918. As Peter Davison says:

If Music Hall did not deal with certain aspects of life, it was I suspect because it did not find them relevant to its experience. Sophisticated political revue must have greater meaning and appeal for those who are involved, or feel involved, in the political struggle than it can for those who feel resigned to be affected by political decisions, but unable to influence them. By and large this was the position of the working class when the Music Halls were at their height.[28]

But if the Music Halls were not engaged politically, they were nevertheless extremely topical, sensitive to, and commenting on current events. Little Tich, the dwarf comedian, chose his stage name because of his resemblance to the notorious Tichbourne Claimant, whose claim that he was the rightful heir to an earldom attracted enormous attention in the 1880s, and whose interminable court cases became a running joke on the Halls. In the same way the militant suffragettes in the decade before the First World War were a constant butt of comedians' humour; even if they were not sympathetically presented, their cause was still pushed into the consciousness of a social group that did not read newspapers or periodicals.

One of the topical issues throughout the whole period of Vesta Tilley's career was the changing position of women, and the whole question of gender roles and expectations. Bessie Bellwood and Jennie Hill (although both have been noted for their 'intense instinct of class consciousness'),[29] Lottie Collins and Marie Lloyd all obviously did not think of themselves as 'political artists' when they extended in their dances and songs the boundaries of the socially permissible, when they exposed over and over again in words and in actions the hypocrisy of the sexual double standard, and when they named themselves in their lives and in their stage personae as autonomous independent women. But in fact Music Hall did a lot, with the can-can, Lottie Collins's extraordinary apache dancing, a stream of male-impersonators, as well as the open sexuality of acts like Marie Lloyd's, to challenge the moralistic taboos of the late Victorian era. The insights of contemporary feminism have certainly taught us that the idea of 'politics' cannot properly be limited to the posturings of the party machines.

It is true that in France, and especially in Paris, sexual politics were much more clearly and explicitly understood at this time, and the acts of Parisian cabaret were more directly concerned with such issues. Mistinguett, perhaps the queen of the French Music Halls, was a personal friend of leading members of the radical intelligensia, including the sculptor Rodin, Oscar Wilde and the young Jean Cocteau. Renoir, Manet, Dégas and above all Toulouse-Lautrec knew well what they were about. Toulouse-Lautrec, despite the opinion of traditionalists who 'accused him of glorifying the grotesque', reflected the sexual freedom, energy and perversity which the French Music Halls chose to present in the form of consciously new types of femaleness: he painted the voluptuous 'La Golue'; Jean Avril who 'had about her an air of depraved virginity . . . the more provocative because she played as a prude, with an assumed modesty, *décolleté* nearly to the waist . . . a creature of cruel moods, cruel passions . . . an absolute passion for her own beauty.'[30] Yvette Gilbert, 'the Sarah Bernhardt of the *café concert*', presented dramatic renderings from the poetry of the new Decadents. There was the heavily charged potency of Mary Hilton, and a great number of other middle-class intellectual women, including Colette, who played Music Hall and found in it intriguing possibilities in their explorations of sexuality.

Actually French standards were not always as open as is often suggested. Colette and her lover the Marquise de Belboeuf once tried to present a sketch in which the Marquise impersonated a male artist infatuated by his model, played by Colette. This mixing of reality and fiction was going too far for her scandalized audience and the curtain had to be rung down to protect the pair of them from physical violence.[31]

But even if English Music Hall was not as conscious of sexual politics as its French counterpart, it still reflected and informed the extraordinary change in the image of women that took place in the years from 1870 to 1914. The New Woman was not just an intellectual construct of some middle-class, nineteenth-century intellectuals; she was everywhere, and changed the image of women throughout all classes of late Victorian society. Even that most conservative of forms, the etiquette book, demonstrates the change. In 1883, Eliza Linton in her *The Girl of the Period* advised her readers that

part of her natural mission is to please and be charming, and she knows that dress sets her off and that men feel more enthusiastically towards her when she is looking fresh and pretty than when she is a dowdy and a fright. And being womanly she likes the admiration of men and thinks their love is a better thing than their indifference. If she likes men she loves children . . . she thinks a happy and populace nursery one of the greatest blessings of her state. . . . She is not above her *métier* as a woman; and she does not want to ape the manliness she can never possess. . . . She has taken it to heart that patience, self-sacrifice, tenderness, quietness . . . modesty . . . are virtues more especially feminine. Passionate ambition, virile energy, the love of strong excitement, self-assertion . . . an undisciplined temper are all qualities that detract from her ideal of womanliness and make her less beautiful than she was meant to be.[32]

But barely fifteen years later, in 1897, an equally conservative and respected writer, Mrs Humphry, was stating in her *Manners for Women*:

The girl of today, with her fine physical development, her bright cheery nature and her robust contempt for all things small and mean is an immense improvement on the girl of yesterday. . . . Instead of maudlin sensibility . . . she has a vigorous contempt for all forms of softness . . . her mind and character are strung up to a firmness of which a sentimental heroine of fifty years ago would have been thoroughly ashamed. . . . She entertains a fine, manly feeling of friendship for her father, and is a good comrade with her brothers, sharing in most of their sports and pastimes. . . . She is thoroughly healthy, and shows it in the elasticity of her steps and the erectness of her carriage . . . in her clear complexion, bright eyes, glossy hair and glowing lips.[33]

And this was the girl that from the 1890s onwards Vesta Tilley presented in humorous extreme; the New Woman — not in the political or intellectual sense, but in the sense of style. She answered the question 'How far can we go?' for a very new group of women; and the answer was funny and by no means repellent to men.

So while Vesta Tilley's male admirers may have adored her because she adored them, and confirmed them in their own sense of inalienable superiority — implying that they were at worst endearingly 'silly' and at best unrecognized heroes, her women fans were getting a very different message. She offered them two, parallel models. First, there was the suggestion that there might be another sort of man, a man who could understand, who could think like a woman, a male sexuality deeply informed and mediated by a female sensibility. She presented a better man than men could ever be, and it was immensely attractive. She also offered a model of where the New Woman might be going — a new sort of possibility for freedom of movement and expression; a woman who could afford to laugh at men while claiming for herself all their privileges. And of course, by ultimately being a nicely married woman, who was rich and successful, famous and beloved, she made that possibility seem quite safe and controlled.

Working-class women responded to her act with a delighted camaraderie. Despite the plaudits of the press, it was not 'The London Idol' that they shouted when she appeared, but 'Good Old Vesta'.

Of a visit she made to Birmingham, Sir Patrick Hannon wrote:

The *women* of Birmingham mobilised themselves in an uproarious welcome . . . Our procession from the Queen's Hotel to the Birmingham Hall was the most striking manifestation of *affection* I have ever seen . . . the streets were blocked with the cheering multitude and mounted policemen found difficulty in providing access to the hall.[34]

Of course her overtly right-wing politics, her refusal to identify herself either with the causes of feminism or of working-class politics; her confinement of sexual daring so rigidly to the stage; her individualism and her satisfaction with a private class transcendence, were all betrayals of the women who made her the star she was. That betrayal is perhaps implicit in the act of male-impersonation. But there was a warmth of response to her act which should not be denied: it was not hysterical, but proud and affectionate. She offered working-class women hope, and a new way of seeing both women and men. And she made them laugh. Any analysis is deficient if it does not acknowledge the pleasure that she gave.

NOTES

Beginners
1. Sheila Rowbotham, *Dreams and Dilemmas*, p. 164, Virago, London, 1983.
2. O. P. Gilbert, *Women in Men's Guise*, p. 171, John Lane, London, 1932.

The Curtain Raiser – Vesta Tilley
1. *The Times*, 14 June 1856.
2. *Punch*, 1862.
3. Henry Mayhew, *Mayhew's London*, (ed.) Peter Quennell, p. 87, Braken Books, London, 1984.
4. Sir Arthur Conan Doyle in the *Era*, 2 July 1912.
5. *The Times*, 2 July 1912.
6. *Evening News*, 23 June 1923.
7. Lady de Frece, *Recollections of Vesta Tilley*, p. 32, Hutchinson, London, 1934.
8. ibid., p. 52.
9. ibid., p. 38.
10. *Dan Leno Hys Book*, p. 36, Greening & Co., London, 1899. (It was long believed that this was a genuine autobiography and is catalogued as such; however, in 1968 it was revealed that it was ghosted by T. C. Elder.)
11. Quoted by Roy Busby in *British Music Hall: An Illustrated Who's Who*, p. 24, Paul Elek, London, 1976.
12. Edgar and Eleanor Johnson (eds.) *The Dickens Theatrical Reader*, p. 403, Gollancz, London, 1964.

13. Quoted by M. Willson Disher in *Winkles and Champagne*, p. 76, Collins, London, 1938.
14. R. Manders and J. Micheson, *British Music Hall*, Hart Davis, London, 1968.
15. Willson Disher, p. 77.
16. *Recollections of Vesta Tilley*, p. 165.
17. O. Stoll, *Post and Mercury*, 9 January 1935.
18. ibid.
19. Willson Disher, p. 78.
20. D. Gilbert, *American Vaudeville: Its Life and Times*, p. 68, Dover Publications, USA, 1940.
21. ibid., p. 69.
22. ibid., p. 69.
23. *Recollections of Vesta Tilley*, p. 187.
24. H. Chance Newton, *Idols of the Halls*, p. 145, Heath Cranton Ltd., London, 1928.
25. *Observer*, 16 April 1919.
26. *Telegraph*, 7 June 1920.
27. *Recollections of Vesta Tilley*, p. 204.

Front Cloth

1. Marina Warner, *Joan of Arc*, p. 156, Weidenfeld & Nicolson, London, 1981.

The Actress in Late Victorian Society

1. F. C. Burnand, 'Behind the Scenes' in *Fortnightly Review*, London, January 1885, p. 89. (Despite his strictures, Burnand twice married actresses.) I am indebted for this quote and for much of the following material to Christopher Kent's article, 'Image and Reality: the Actress and Society', in Martha Vicinus (ed.), *A Widening Sphere*, Indiana University Press, 1977.
2. See Yvonne Kapp, *Eleanor Marx*, vol. i, pp. 24 and 234–5, Lawrence & Wishart, London, 1972.
3. George Rowell, *The Victorian Theatre*, p. 9, Oxford University Press, London, 1956.
4. Sir Theodore Martin, *Helena Faucit (Lady Martin)*, p. 166, Blackwood & Sons, London, 1900.
5. ibid., p. 125.
6. Quoted by C. Kent, p. 108.

7. Mary Jeune, Lady St Helier, *Memories of Fifty Years*, p. 189, Edward Arnold, London, 1909.
8. Edgar and Eleanor Johnson (eds.), *The Dickens Theatrical Reader*, p. 310, London, 1964.
9. Rowell, p. 76.
10. ibid., p. 78.
11. T. H. S. Escott, 'A Foreign Resident' in *Society in London*, p. 169, Chatto & Windus, London, 1885.
12. Kate Phillips, quoted by C. Kent, p. 111 (see note 1).
13. *Telegraph*, 12 June 1920, quoted in Lady de Frece, *Recollections of Vesta Tilley*, p. 204, Hutchinson, London, 1934.
14. *Recollections*, p. 121.
15. Roy Busby, *British Music Hall: An Illustrated Who's Who*, p. 24, Paul Elek, London, 1976.
16. ibid., p. 39.
17. Leslie Fiedler, *Freaks*, p. 181, Simon & Schuster, USA, 1978.

The Woman Drag Artist

1. Virginia Woolf, *Orlando*, p. 117, Granada, London, 1977 (first published by the Hogarth Press, London, 1928).
2. Marina Warner, *Joan of Arc*, p. 157, Weidenfeld & Nicolson, London, 1981.
3. ibid., p. 75.
4. O. P. Gilbert, *Women in Men's Guise*, p. 64, John Lane, London, 1932.
5. Peter Ackroyd, *Dressing Up*, p. 77, Thames & Hudson, London, 1979.
6. A. J. Merck, 'The City's Achievements' in Sue Lipshitz (ed.), *Tearing the Veil: Essays in Femininity*, p. 112, Routledge & Kegan Paul, London, 1978.
7. Esther Newton, *Mother Camp*, p. 28, University of Chicago Press, London, 1972, 1979.
8. Ackroyd, p. 98.
9. Oscar Wilde, 'The truth of masks' in *Intentions*, p. 231, James Osgood, McIlvaine & Co., London, 1891.
10. Roland Barthes, *Le Plaisir du texte*, Seuil, France, 1973.
11. *Tootsie*, directed by Sydney Pollock, Columbia Pictures, 1982.
12. Annette Kuhn, 'Sexual Disguise and Cinema'. To be published in a collection of essays in 1986 by Routledge & Kegan Paul,

London. My debt to Kuhn's analysis of performance drag is extensive. I thank her for allowing me access to her paper.

13. Mary Frith, *The Life and Death of Mrs Mary Frith*. Mary Frith was born in 1589. Her life is well-recorded by her contemporaries and she was persecuted during the Puritan Interregnum.

14. Marina Warner, *Joan of Arc*, p. 145, Weidenfeld & Nicolson, London, 1981.

15. ibid., pp. 145–6.

16. See for example, *Indiana* (1832) and *Lélia* (1833).

17. Jane W. Stedman, 'From Dame to Woman: W. S. Gilbert and Theatrical Transvestism' in Martha Vicinus (ed.), *Suffer and Be Still*, p. 21, Indiana University Press, 1972.

18. ibid., p. 20 and notes.

19. Esther Newton, p. 75.

20. Diana Simmonds, in discussion with the author, 1985.

21. Joan Rivière, 'Womanliness as Masquerade' in *International Journal of Psychoanalysis*, vol. x (1929), pp. 306–7.

Finale

1. Oscar Wilde, *A Few Maxims for the Instruction of the Over-educated*.

2. Oswald Stoll's Introduction in Lady de Frece, *Recollections of Vesta Tilley*, p. 9, Hutchinson, London, 1934.

3. P. Davison, *Songs of the British Music Hall*, USA, 1971.

4. ibid.

5. H. Chance Newton, *Idols of the Halls*, p. 123, Heath Cranton, London, 1928. (Newton worked for Vesta Tilley, creating sketches and a burlesque *Cartouche and Company*, in which she was to have played one of her rare female roles in 1891. The tour of this show, for which she and Walter de Frece had created their own company was interrupted by her illness. Newton was an outrageous gossip, and a number of Vesta Tilley anecdotes, including the information that Oswald Stoll was in love with her, seem to stem from him.)

6. St John Irving, in the *Observer*, 22 April 1934. This review of *Recollections* is an extremely useful article for corroborating factual details of her life, and for a late impression of her skill.

7. *Observer*, 2 July 1920.

8. Sir Alfred Butt, Bt. MP, 'An Appreciation' from *Recollections*, p. 9.

9. W. R. Titterton, *From Theatre to Music Hall*, p. 147, Stephen Swift & Co., London, 1912.

10. *Francis & Day's Album of Vesta Tilley's Popular Songs*, Francis Day & Hunter, London, no date. Francis Day & Hunter (whose shop, now called FDH Records, is still open on the Charing Cross Road) were one of the principal sheet music publishers of the 1890s and 1900s. Their covers are particularly fine period pieces; the Victoria & Albert Museum has a large selection. As with many Music Hall songs there are slightly differing versions of this song available.

11. Individual Song Sheet, in Victoria & Albert Theatre Museum, no date.

12. In *Francis and Day's Album*.

13. Willson Disher, *Winkles and Champagne*, p. 78, Collins, London, 1938.

14. In *Recollections*, p. 134.

15. ibid., p. 133.

16. Titterton, p. 147.

17. In *Recollections*, p. 136.

18. G. Sudworth, *The Great Little Tilley*, p. 122, Courtney Publications, UK, 1984.

19. ibid., p. 136.

20. ibid., p. 135.

21. Titterton, p. 146.

22. Willson Disher, p. 80.

23. 'A Bohemian Journalist', *The World's Idol. Queen of Varietyland. An Illustrated Souvenir of Vesta Tilley: An Impression of a Great Artiste*, no publisher, no date, p. 4.

24. According to J. Manders, in personal communication with the author.

25. Esther Newton, *Mother Camp*, p. 52, University of Chicago Press, London, 1972, 1979.

26. A personal communication, anonymous by request, to the author.

27. All songs in the paragraph quoted under the name of the singer in Roy Busby, *British Music Hall: An Illustrated Who's Who*, Paul Elek, London, 1975.

28. P. Davison, p. 17.

29. Harold Scot, quoted in Roy Busby, *British Music Hall: An Illustrated Who's Who*, p. 78, Paul Elek, London, 1976.
30. Arthur Symons in *The Yellow Book*, quoted in P. Leslie, *A Hard Act to Follow*, p. 94, Paddington Press, London, 1978.
31. ibid., p. 139.
32. Eliza Linton, *The Girl of the Period*, 1883, quoted in P. Hollis, *Women in Public*, Allen & Unwin, London, p. 20.
33. Mrs Humphry, *Manners for Women*, pp. 4 and 5, London, 1897.
34. *The Times*, 10 October 1952 (my emphases).

BIBLIOGRAPHY

Autobiography

de Frece, Lady V., *Recollections of Vesta Tilley*, Hutchinson, London, 1934

Books about Vesta Tilley

'A Bohemian Journalist', *The World's Idol. Queen of Varietyland. Illustrated Souvenir of Vesta Tilley: An Impression of a Great Artiste*, no publisher, no date

Francis and Day, *Francis and Day's Album of Vesta Tilley's Popular Songs*, with a biographical sketch by Charles Wilmott, and the songs: 'Jolly Good Luck to the Girl who Loves a Soldier'; 'I Know my Business'; 'By the Sad Sea Waves'; 'I'm the Idol of the Girls'; 'That's the Time a Fellow Wants His Ma'; 'When a Fellah has Turned Sixteen'; 'It's Part of a P'liceman's Duty'; 'Following a Fellah with a Face Like Me'; 'S—U—N—D—A—Y'; 'The Pretty Little Maidie's Sea-Trip'; 'Who Said "Girls"?'; 'Give it to Father'; 'Some Danced the Lancers'; 'After the Ball'; 'Algy, the Piccadilly Johnny'; 'The Midnight Son'; 'Following in Father's Footsteps', Francis, Day & Hunter, London, no date

Sudworth, G., *The Great Little Tilley*, Courtney Publications, Luton, 1984

Selected background material

Ackroyd, P., *Dressing Up*, Thames & Hudson, London, 1979

Busby, R., *British Music Hall: An Illustrated Who's Who*, Paul Elek, London, 1976

Davison, P., *Songs of the British Music Hall*, Oak Publications, USA, 1971

Gilbert, D., *American Vaudeville: Its Life and Times*, Dover Publications, USA, 1940

Gilbert, O. P., *Women in Men's Guise*, London, 1932

Leslie, P., *A Hard Act to Follow*, Paddington Press, London, 1978

Mander, R. and Micheson, J., *British Music Hall*, Hart Davis, London, 1968

Newton, E., *Mother Camp*, University of Chicago Press, London, 1972, 1979

Vicinus, M. (ed.), *A Widening Sphere: Changing Roles of Victorian Women*, Indiana University Press, USA, 1977

Woolf, V., *Orlando*, Granada, London, 1977 (first published by the Hogarth Press, 1928)

Other materials

Recordings

Few recordings are publicly available; however, both Decca and the World Record Club have reissued on LP albums of Music Hall songs recorded by their original artists. *Top of the Bill*, World Record Club, SHB 22, includes two of her songs

Film

After the Ball, a biographical film, directed by Compton Bennett; screenplay by Hubert Gregg and Peter Blackmore; produced by Peter Rogers; starring Pat Kirkwood as Vesta Tilley, and Lawrence Hervey as Walter de Frece, London, 1957

Radio

'A Tribute to Vesta Tilley', Midland Home Service, May 1964

Stage

Music Hall Extravaganza, based on the iife and times of Vesta Tilley, directed by John Doyle, the Swan Theatre, Worcester, May 1981

INDEX